THE BIG GREEN SALAD BOOK

Ann Lerman

Illustrations by Teresa Anderko

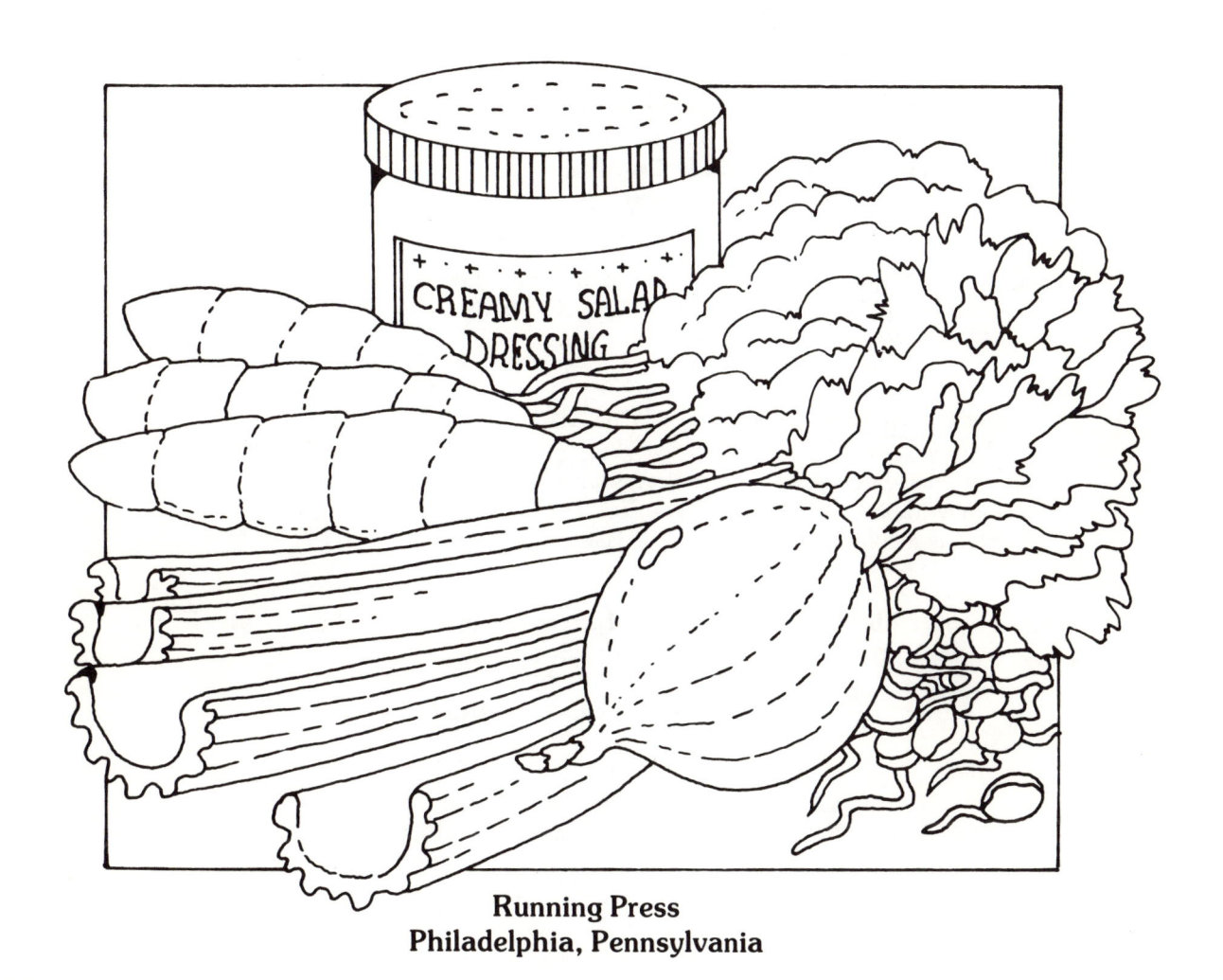

Running Press
Philadelphia, Pennsylvania

Copyright © 1977 Running Press

Printed in the United States of America

All rights reserved under the Pan American and International Copyright Conventions

Canadian representatives: John Wiley & Sons Canada, Ltd.
22 Worcester Road, Rexdale, Ontario M9W 1L1

International representatives: Kaiman & Polon, Inc.
2175 Lemoine Avenue, Fort Lee, New Jersey 07024

9 8 7 6 5 4
Digit on right indicates the number of this printing.

Library of Congress Cataloging in Publication Data

Lerman, Ann, 1942 —
   The Big Green Salad Book.

Includes index.
SUMMARY: Includes recipes for a wide variety of salads and dressings.
1. Salads. [1. Salads] I. Title.
TX807.L42   641.8'3   77-4306
ISBN 0-914294-90-3 Paperback
ISBN 0-914294-89-X Library binding

Cover and interior illustration by Teresa Anderko
Cover Design by Jim Wilson
Interior art direction by Linda Grossman
Edited by Peter J. Dorman

Back Cover text reproduced: By permission. From Webster's Third New International Dictionary © 1976 by G. & C. Merriam Co., Publishers of the Merriam-Webster Dictionaries.

Typeface: Souvenir; Composition by Comp•Art, Inc., Philadelphia, Pennsylvania
Cover printed by Harrison Color Process Lithographers, Willow Grove, Pennsylvania
Printed and bound by Port City Press, Baltimore, Maryland

This book may be ordered directly from the publisher.
Please include 25c postage.

Try your bookstore first.

Running Press
38 South Nineteenth Street
Philadelphia, Pennsylvania 19103

First Words

Salads were traditionally served as accompaniments to main dishes. Now, it seems, they are coming into their own. There is no healthier way to live than to eat lots of fruits and vegetables. Because salads are good for you doesn't mean that they have to be dull and uninspired. Use your imagination when preparing any of the recipes in this book. Enjoy trying a new dressing or adding an additional ingredient for taste or color. Salads can look as good as they taste.

Most salads are simple and quick to make. There are a few basic tools that you need. The *knife*, one of your most important tools, is of several sorts. A paring knife, 3 to 3½ inches long, is used for peeling, paring, and cutting small fruits and vegetables. A utility knife, 5 to 7 inches long, is used for peeling, paring, and chopping in heavier jobs involving large fruits and vegetables. A chopping knife has a wide, 8-inch blade, and is used for chopping, mincing, and dicing fruits and vegetables. The curved grapefruit knife is used for removing sections from citrus fruits.

There are many tools to help you in cutting and chopping chores. Here are some of the most useful.

A *grater* is used for grating and slicing. Get a model that stands upright with several sizes of teeth and a slicer. *Kitchen shears*, for snipping herbs and every kind of kitchen cutting, should be sturdy and feel comfortable. *Meat grinders* are for grinding nuts and vegetables as well as meat. Get a metal grinder that clamps to a table or counter. A *chopping board* should be used for every chore that requires a cutting surface; 16 x 20 inches is a good size. Make sure it is made of a durable hardwood, such as maple or oak, with a thickness of three-fourths to 1 inch.

For every form of mixing and measuring you will need a few essentials. An electric *blender* and/or rotary *beater*, for thoroughly beating dressings and sauces, is invaluable. *Wooden spoons* should be used for creaming, beating, and stirring; get a variety of sizes. Wooden spoons are better than metal because they move easily along the curved sides of the bowl. *Measuring spoons* are necessary for measuring both dry and liquid ingredients. Get at least one standard set, which includes a quarter teaspoon, a half-teaspoon, a full teaspoon, and one tablespoon. And *measuring cups*, for measuring both dry and liquid ingredients, should be purchased in a set of graduated sizes in either glass, pottery, or stainless steel. One more indispensable tool, a *rubber spatula*, is good for folding foods as well as scraping the sides of a mixing bowl.

Purchase fruits and vegetables that look delicious. In most cases avoid blemishes, bruises, and broken skin. Ripe, fresh fruit should be used as soon as possible. Ripen fruit at room temperature and store it in a refrigerator. Never wash fruits or vegetables until you are ready to use them. And remember, washing before storage will promote decay. Wrap vegetables in plastic wrap and keep refrigerated until ready to use.

Herbs are the leaves or the seeds and flowers of aromatic plants. Fresh herbs are preferable since dried ones may lose their aroma. If you are using dried herbs, use only about half as much as when using fresh herbs; and soak dried herbs before using. Store dried herbs in airtight containers kept in a cool place.

Spices are the roots, barks, stems, buds, seeds, or fruits of aromatic tropical plants. They should be purchased in small quantities because they tend to lose their flavor quickly.

Serve salads on a chilled salad plate or bowl. Glass serving pieces complement your salad by allowing all its color and texture to be seen. When preparing a salad that calls for rubbing the bowl with a garlic clove, a wooden bowl is needed.

Enjoy preparing your salads. Keep them simple, neat, and yet interesting. To enhance their appearance, garnish your salads with almost anything from almonds to zinnias. It has been said that we eat with our eyes as well as our palate. A variety of shapes and colors will make your salads an all-around enjoyable experience.

—Annie Lerman

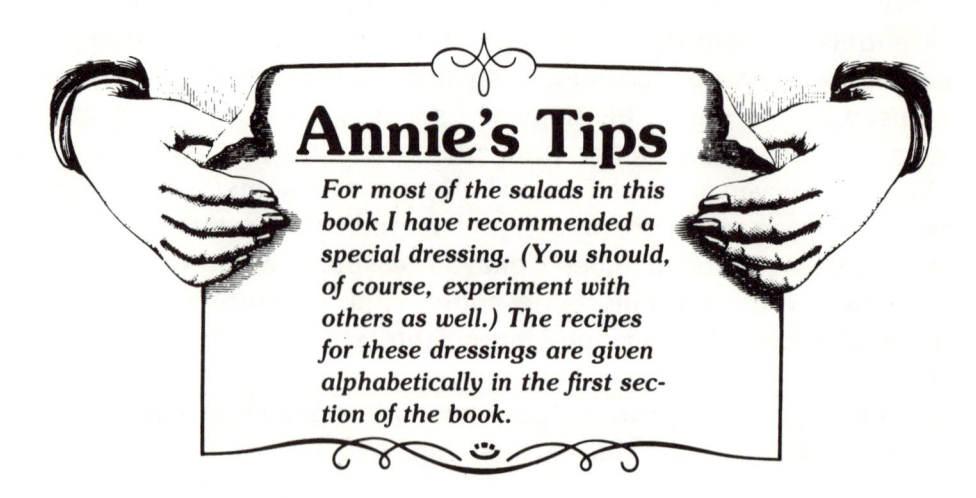

Annie's Tips

For most of the salads in this book I have recommended a special dressing. (You should, of course, experiment with others as well.) The recipes for these dressings are given alphabetically in the first section of the book.

Contents

First Words . . . . **v**

Glossary of Terms . . . . **xi**

DRESSINGS **15**

Avocado Dressing • Beet Dressing • Caper Dressing • Cheese and Lemon Dressing • Citrus Dressing • Cool Cucumber Sauce • Cream Cheese Dressing • Creamy Bacon Dressing • Creamy Salad Dressing • Dill Sour Cream Dressing • Fines Herbes Vinaigrette • French Mustard Dressing • French-Style Blue Cheese Dressing • Fresh Fruit Dressing • Ginger Cheese Dressing • Ginger Dressing • Herbed Sour Cream Dressing • Honey French Dressing • Horseradish Dressing • Lemon-Cucumber Dressing • Lemon Dressing • Mocha Dressing • Molasses Dressing • Orange-Honey Fruit Dressing • Oriental Dressing • Parmesan Dressing Rosé • Peppered Avocado Dressing • Pickled Beet Sour Cream Dressing • Pineapple Salad Dressing • Quick Potato Salad Dressing • Sour Cream Slaw Dressing • Special Yogurt Dressing • Strawberry Dressing • Sweet Yogurt Dressing • Tangy Tomato Dressing • Tarragon Sour Cream Dressing • Tomato Honey Dressing • Two-Cheese Dressing • White Wine Dressing • Wine Dressing • Yogurt Dressing Supreme • Yogurt Slaw Dressing • Zesty Blue Cheese Dressing

BIG GREEN SALADS 45

Asparagus and Mushroom Salad • Avocado Gazpacho Salad • Avocado Spinach Salad • Bean Sprout and Cucumber Salad • Bean Sprout and Mushroom Salad • Beet Salad • Broccoli-Tomato Salad • Buz's Mixed Seafood Salad • Cauliflower Salad • Celery Slaw • Cheese Spinach Salad • Chicken and Ham Salad • Crab Salad • Cucumber-Radish Salad • Cucumber and Shrimp Salad • Gazpacho Salad • Green Salad with Hard-Boiled Egg • Japanese Salad • Marinated Avocado-Mushroom Salad • Marinated Zucchini with Tomato Salad • Mixed Salad • Mushroom and Bacon Salad • Sesame Lettuce Salad • Special Green Salad • Special Tossed Romaine • Sweet Pepper Salad • Tomato-Beef Salad • Tomato Salad Rosé • Tomatoes Stuffed with Beets • Tomatoes Stuffed with Shrimp Salad • Tuna Salad in Pepper Cups • Vegetable Salad Plate with Dip • Vegetable-Shrimp Salad

FRUIT SALADS 71

Apple-Raisin Slaw • Bananas and Pears with Port • Banana Split Salad • Beet Fruit Salad • Cheese and Fruit Salad • Citrus Salad • Cream Cheese Fruit Salad • Fruit Salad Platter • Fruit Salad with Shrimp • Ginger Summer Salad • Holiday Fruit Salad • Molasses-Citrus Salad • Pineapple Salad with Crab • Poached Naval Orange Salad • Strawberry Delight • Stuffed Peach Salad • Stuffed Pear Salad • Tossed Fruit Salad • Yam-Fruit Salad

SALADS MADE WITH POTATOES, RICE, AND PASTA 87

Apple Raisin Potato Salad • Bologna Salad • Chicken and Brown Rice Toss • Chicken-Potato Salad • French Fry Potato Salad • French-Style Green Bean and Potato Salad • Garden Macaroni Salad • Hot Potato Salad • Macaroni and Cheese Salad • Macaroni and Cheese Salad Ring • Macaroni Slaw • Pepper Steak Salad • Sweetcorn Salad • Tuna-Fruit Sea-shell Salad • Turkey and Garbanzo Bean Toss • Vegetable Rice Salad

SALADS MADE IN MOLDS 103

Avocado-Tuna Salad Ring • Beet Cucumber Salad Ring • Cider Salad Mold • Cottage Cheese Peach Salad • Cran-Apple Turkey Salad Mold • Cucumber and Grape Salad • Frozen Fruitcake Salad • Fruit Squares • Grapefruit Ring • Lime-Walnut Salad • Molded Vegetable Salad • Molded Waldorf Salad • Pear Cucumber Mold • Pear and Lime Salad Mold • Red Top Egg Salad • Sangria Salad • Seafood Salad • Spiced Peach Salad • Strawberry Yogurt Mold • Tomato Ring

Index 123

Glossary of Terms

Beat: to mix ingredients together with a circular up-and-down motion, using a whisk, a spoon, or a rotary electric beater.

Blend: to stir, rather than beat, the ingredients until they are thoroughly combined.

Brush on: to apply a liquid to the surface of food with a small brush.

Chill: to make cold, not frozen, in a refrigerator.

Chop: to cut into small pieces.

Coat: to cover food lightly but thoroughly with either a liquid or dry substance.

Combine: to mix or blend together two or more ingredients.

Core: to remove the inedible central portion of certain fruits and vegetables.

Crisp: to make firm (leafy vegetables such as lettuce are washed, dried, and chilled).

Cube: to cut into small, equal-sized squares, generally one-quarter to one-half inch.

Dice: to cut into very small even cubes.

Dissolve: to make a solution by adding liquid to a solid substance or by heating a solid until it melts.

Drain: to remove liquid, usually by allowing food to stand in a strainer or collander until liquid has drained off.

Fines herbes: a mixture of minced herbs — parsley, chives, tarragon — used to flavor foods.

Flake: to break into small pieces with a fork, as with cooked fish.

Fold: to add or mix by gently turning one part over another with a spoon.

Garnish: to decorate or accompany a dish by adding other food stuffs, such as parsley or flowers.

Grate: to reduce a food to small particles by rubbing it on the teeth of a grater.

Grind: to reduce foods like herbs and spices to a fine, powdery consistency using a mortar and pestle.

Hull: to remove the calyx, or hull, of certain fruits such as the strawberry and raspberry.

Julienne: food such as carrots or cheese cut into thin, matchlike strips.

Marinade: a liquid in which food is placed to enhance its flavor and to make it more tender.

Marinate: to let stand in a seasoned vinegar-oil mixture.
Mash: to soften and break down food by using the back of a spoon or by forcing through a ricer.
Mince: to cut or chop into very fine pieces
Mix: to blend or stir together two or more ingredients.
Pare: to remove the outer covering and stem of a fruit or vegetable with a knife or other peeling tool.
Partially set: having the consistency of unbeaten egg whites.
Pith: the white membrane under the rind of citrus fruits.
Rind: the outer skin of a fruit or vegetable.
Sauté: to cook food briefly in a small amount of hot fat.
Set: used in reference to liquids which have congealed and retained their shape.
Steam: to cook by means of vapor from a boiling liquid rising through the food.
Unmold: to remove from a mold.

THE BIG GREEN SALAD BOOK

DRESSINGS

Avocado Dressing

1 ripe avocado, peeled and seeded
4 tablespoons mayonnaise
2 tablespoons lemon juice
1/2 teaspoon salt
1/2 teaspoon horseradish
1/8 teaspoon cayenne
1 clove garlic (optional)

Mash avocado and lemon juice with fork until smooth. Mix in mayonnaise, horseradish, and cayenne. Squeeze garlic through press. Mix all ingredients well. Add salt to taste.
    Serve with tossed salad greens or tomato and lettuce.

Annie's Tips
Yield of avocado dressing will vary with size of avocado.

Beet Dressing

1 cooked beet, diced
1 slice   onion, minced
1 cup salad oil
2 tablespoons lemon juice

1/4 teaspoon tarragon
1/4 teaspoon dried mustard
1 teaspoon salt
1 small hard-boiled egg, minced

Mix all ingredients together by hand. Chill well before serving. Makes about 1 1/2 cups.
Serve with tossed green salad.

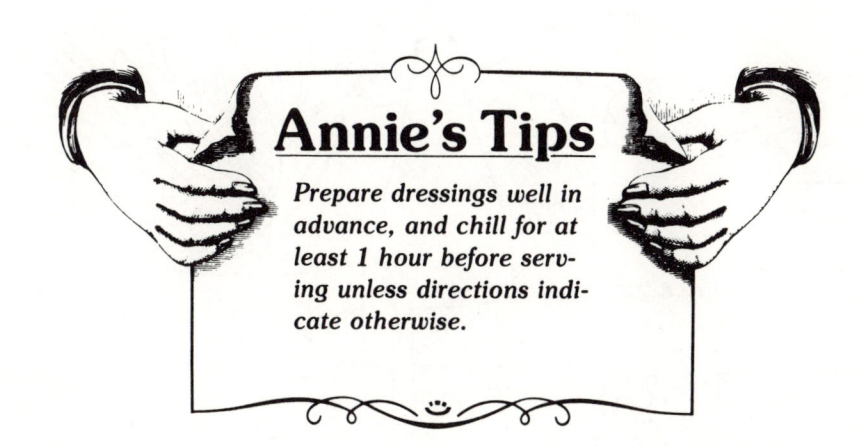

Annie's Tips

Prepare dressings well in advance, and chill for at least 1 hour before serving unless directions indicate otherwise.

Caper Dressing

1/4 cup capers, drained
1/3 cup salad oil
1/4 cup tarragon vinegar
2 tablespoons dry white wine

1 teaspoon sugar
1/2 teaspoon salt
1/2 teaspoon dry mustard
freshly ground pepper

If capers are large, cut in half. In screw-top jar combine all ingredients. Cover and shake.

Makes 1 cup.

Serve with salad greens or vegetable salad.

Cheese and Lemon Dressing

4 ounces blue cheese, crumbled
1/4 teaspoon grated lemon rind
1/4 cup lemon juice

3/4 cup salad oil
1 teaspoon salt
1 cup dairy sour cream

Blend all ingredients except sour cream in blender or electric mixer. Add sour cream and stir until blended. Chill before serving.
   Makes 2 cups.
   Serve with seafood or mixed salad greens.

Citrus Dressing

1/4 cup sugar
1 teaspoon salt
1 teaspoon paprika

1 teaspoon dry mustard
1/3 cup lime juice
2/3 cup salad oil

Blend all ingredients in electric blender for 15 seconds on high speed.
   Makes 1 1/2 cups.
   Serve on citrus salad or avocado salad.

Cool Cucumber Sauce

1/2 cup mayonnaise
1/2 cup lemon yogurt
1/2 cup cucumber, chopped
1 tablespoon chives, chopped
1 teaspoon chopped parsley
1/4 teaspoon salt
1/4 teaspoon dill weed

Combine all ingredients. Mix well. Chill before serving.
  Makes 1 1/2 cups.
  Serve with fresh vegetable salad or molded salad.

Cream Cheese Dressing

one 3-ounce package cream
  cheese, softened
1 tablespoon honey
1/4 teaspoon salt
2 teaspoons lemon juice
1/4 cup orange juice

Combine cream cheese with honey and salt. Add lemon juice and orange juice and beat with electric mixer until smooth. Chill before serving.
  Makes 3/4 cup.
  Serve on fruit salad.

Creamy Bacon Dressing

2 tablespoons lemon juice
1/2 cup mayonnaise
1 tablespoon honey
1/8 teaspoon salt
4 slices crisp bacon, crumbled
2 tablespoons onion, finely chopped

Add lemon juice to mayonnaise. Stir remaining ingredients. Makes 3/4 cup.

Serve immediately on spinach or tossed salad greens.

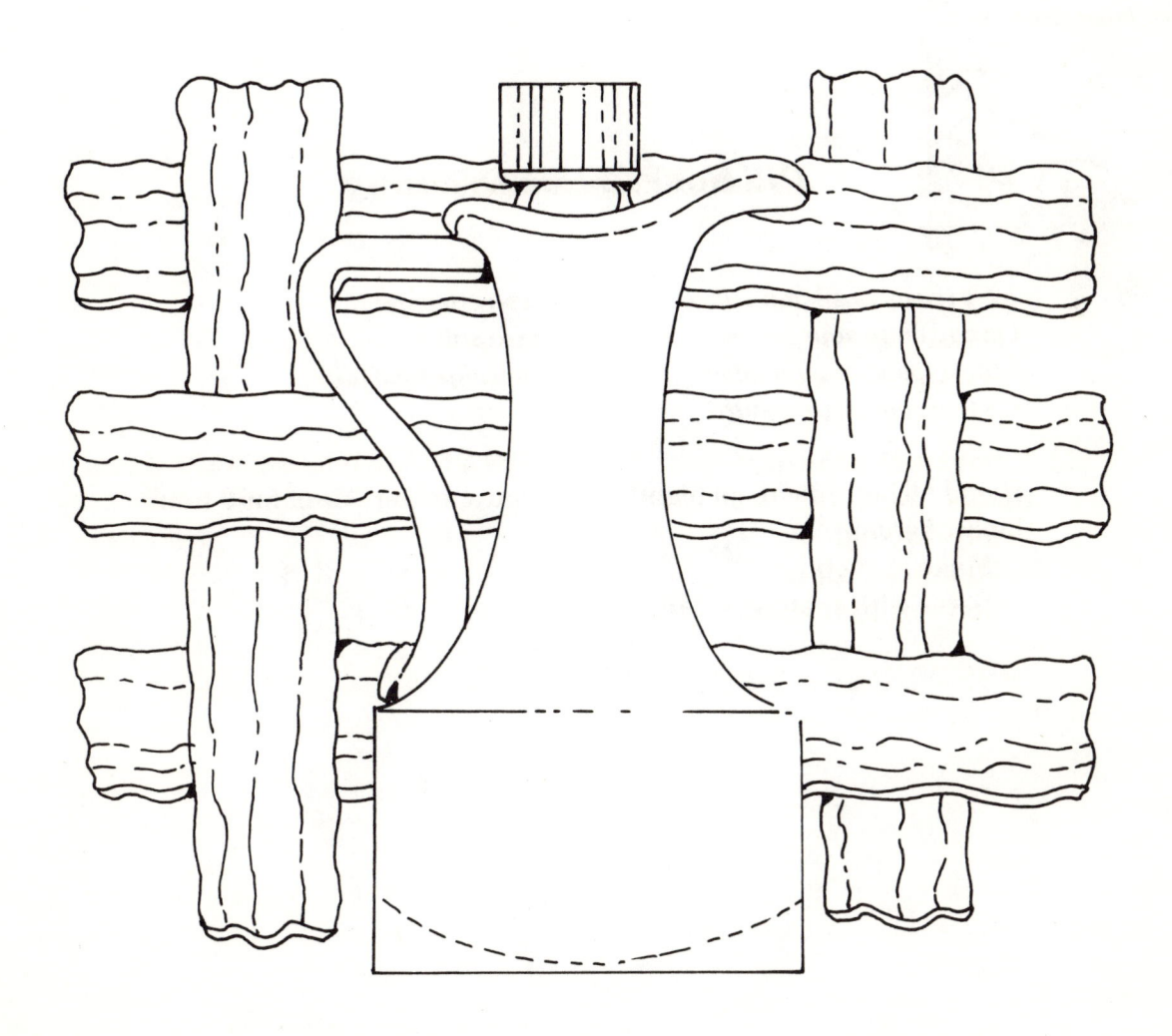

Creamy Salad Dressing

1/2 cup mayonnaise
1 cup dairy sour cream
1/2 cup parsley sprigs, stems removed, minced well
2 tablespoons vinegar
1 teaspoon Worcestershire sauce
1/2 teaspoon salt
1 onion, finely chopped
1 cup pitted ripe olives, chopped, drained

Blend all ingredients except onion and olives in blender or electric mixer. Add onions and olives.
    Makes about 1 1/2 cups.
    Serve on vegetable or potato salad.

Annie's Tips
Try substituting the suggested dressing with your own favorite dressing.

Dill Sour Cream Dressing

1 1/2 teaspoons lemon juice
1/2 cup dairy sour cream
1 tablespoon mayonnaise
1/8 teaspoon dry mustard
dash cayenne
dash salt
2 springs fresh dill

Blend all ingredients in blender or electric mixer. Chill for 2 hours before serving.
    Makes 1/2 cup.
    Serve with seafood salad.

Fines Herbes Vinaigrette

*1 teaspoon fresh chives,
  finely chopped*
*1 tablespoon fresh parsley,
  finely chopped*
*1 teaspoon prepared French
  mustard*
1 garlic clove, crushed
1/2 teaspoon salt
12 tablespoons olive oil
4 tablespoons tarragon vinegar
2 tablespoons lemon juice
*1/4 teaspoon black pepper,
  freshly ground*

In small mixing bowl, using a wooden spoon, combine chives, parsley, mustard, salt, pepper, and garlic. Gradually stir 3 tablespoons olive oil. Transfer mixture to screw-top jar. Add remaining olive oil, vinegar, and lemon juice. Cover and shake.
  Makes 1 cup.
  Serve on tossed salad greens or tomato salad.

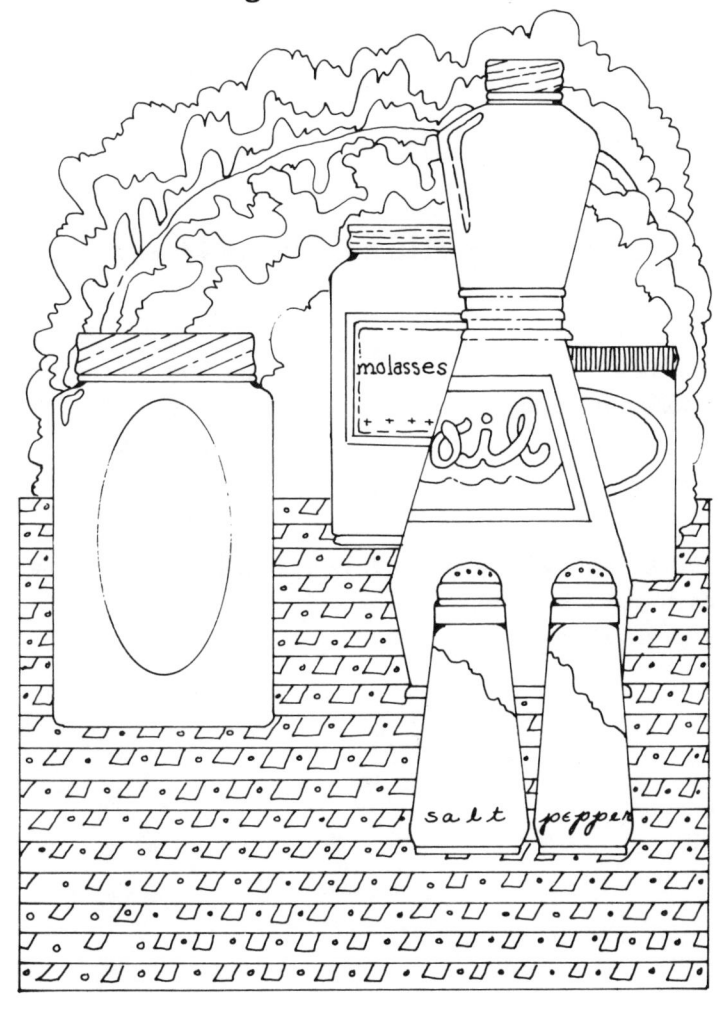

French Mustard Dressing

2 full teaspoons Grey Poupon® mustard
1/2 teaspoon salt
1/3 cup red wine vinegar, scant
1/3 cup corn oil, scant
1/4 teaspoon black pepper

In screw-top jar combine all ingredients. Cover and shake well.
Makes about 3/4 cup.
Serve with tomatoes marinated in dressing.

French-Style Blue Cheese Dressing

1 cup salad oil
3 tablespoons lemon juice
1 teaspoon sugar
1/2 teaspoon salt
4 ounces blue cheese, crumbled
2 teaspoons paprika
1 slice onion, mined

Mix all ingredients with electric mixer. Chill well before serving.
Makes about 1 1/2 cups.
Serve with salad greens.

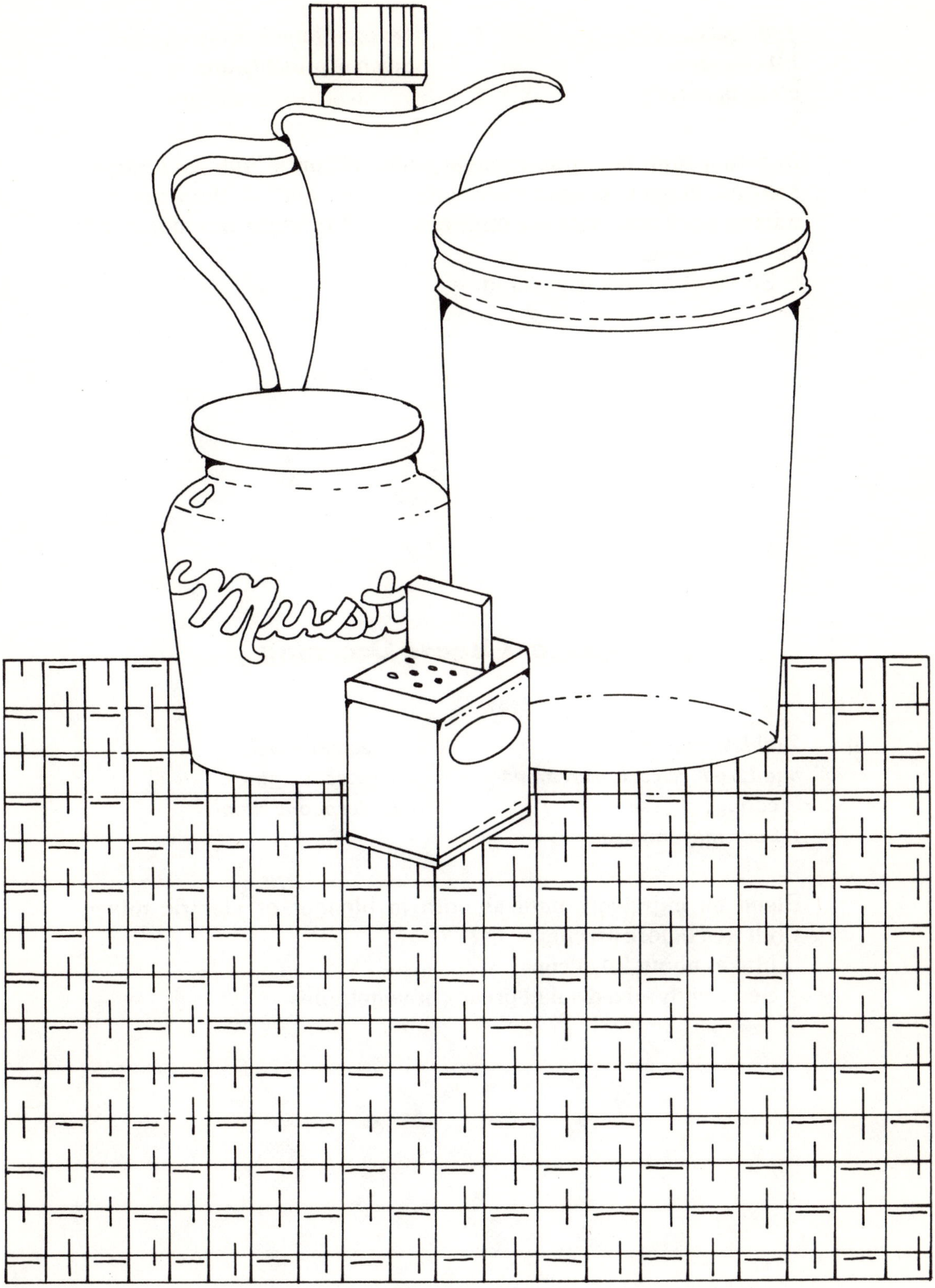
Must

Fresh Fruit Dressing

4 egg yolks
1/4 cup sugar
pinch of salt

1/4 cup Marsala wine
pinch of ground nutmeg

In a saucepan beat yolks, sugar, and salt until light and lemon-colored. Place saucepan over boiling water and continue beating, adding wine and nutmeg until thick and mixture mounds. Chill before serving.
    Serve with fresh fruit salad.

Ginger Cheese Dressing

2 tablespoons milk
one 12-ounce carton creamed
   cottage cheese
1/2 cup mayonnaise

1/4 teaspoon salt
1/2 teaspoon ginger
2 tablespoons sugar

Blend all ingreients until smooth in blender or electric mixer. Chill well before serving.
    Makes about 2 1/4 cups.
    Serve with mixed salad greens or vegetables.

Ginger Dressing

1 small clove garlic
1 tablespoon fresh ginger, chopped

1 strip lemon peel
1/2 cup sesame seed oil
1 cup rice vinegar

Put all ingredients into blender. Blend to creamy stage.
Makes 1 1/2 cups.
Serve with tossed salad greens.

Herbed Sour Cream Dressing

1 cup dairy sour cream
2 tablespoons red wine vinegar
1 teaspoon sugar

1/2 teaspoon salt
1/2 teaspoon celery seed
1/4 teaspoon thyme

Mix all ingredients until well blended. Chill before serving.
Makes about 1 cup.
Serve with seafood salad.

Honey French Dressing

3/4 cup salad oil
1/4 cup lemon juice
1/2 cup honey
1/2 teaspoon Worcestershire
3/4 teaspoon salt

1/4 teaspoon pepper
1/4 teaspoon paprika
1/4 teaspoon dry mustard
1/2 teaspoon celery seed
small piece lemon rind

Put all ingredients in blender. Blend until smooth.
    Makes 1 1/2 cups.
    Serve with tossed salad green or vegetable salad.

Horseradish Dressing

1 cup mayonnaise
1/2 cup buttermilk
2 tablespoons green onion,
 finely chopped

1 1/2 tablespoons horseradish
1/2 teaspoon salt
1/8 teaspoon white pepper

Combine all ingredients. Chill before serving.
 Makes 1 2/3 cups.
 Serve with vegetable salad with beef.

Lemon-Cucumber Dressing

1 cup mayonnaise
1 cup cucumber, seeded and
 finely chopped
2 tablespoons lemon juice

1 tablespoon onion, minced
2 tablespoons grated lemon peel
1 teaspoon salt
1 cup plain yogurt

Combine all ingredients, except yogurt. Fold in yogurt. Chill before serving.
 Makes 2 1/2 cups.
 Serve over greens.

Lemon Dressing

1 cup mayonnaise
1 tablespoon grated lemon peel
2 teaspoons celery seed
1 cup lemon yogurt

Combine lemon peel and celery seed with mayonnaise. Fold yogurt into mayonnaise mixture. Chill before serving.
    Makes 2 cups.
    Serve on vegetable salad or fruit salad.

Mocha Dressing

1 cup coffee yogurt
1 tablespoon cocoa, sifted
1 tablespoon honey
1/4 teaspoon cinnamon

Combine cocoa, honey, and cinnamon with yogurt in small bowl. Stir to blend. Chill before serving.
    Makes 1 cup.
    Serve on fruit salad.

Molasses Dressing

2/3 cup salad oil
1/2 cup lime juice
2 tablespoons molasses
1 teaspoon white pepper
1 teaspoon salt
1 teaspoon dry mustard

Combine all ingredients in screw-top jar. Cover and shake thoroughly.
    Makes about 1 1/2 cups.
    Serve on citrus salad or avocado salad.

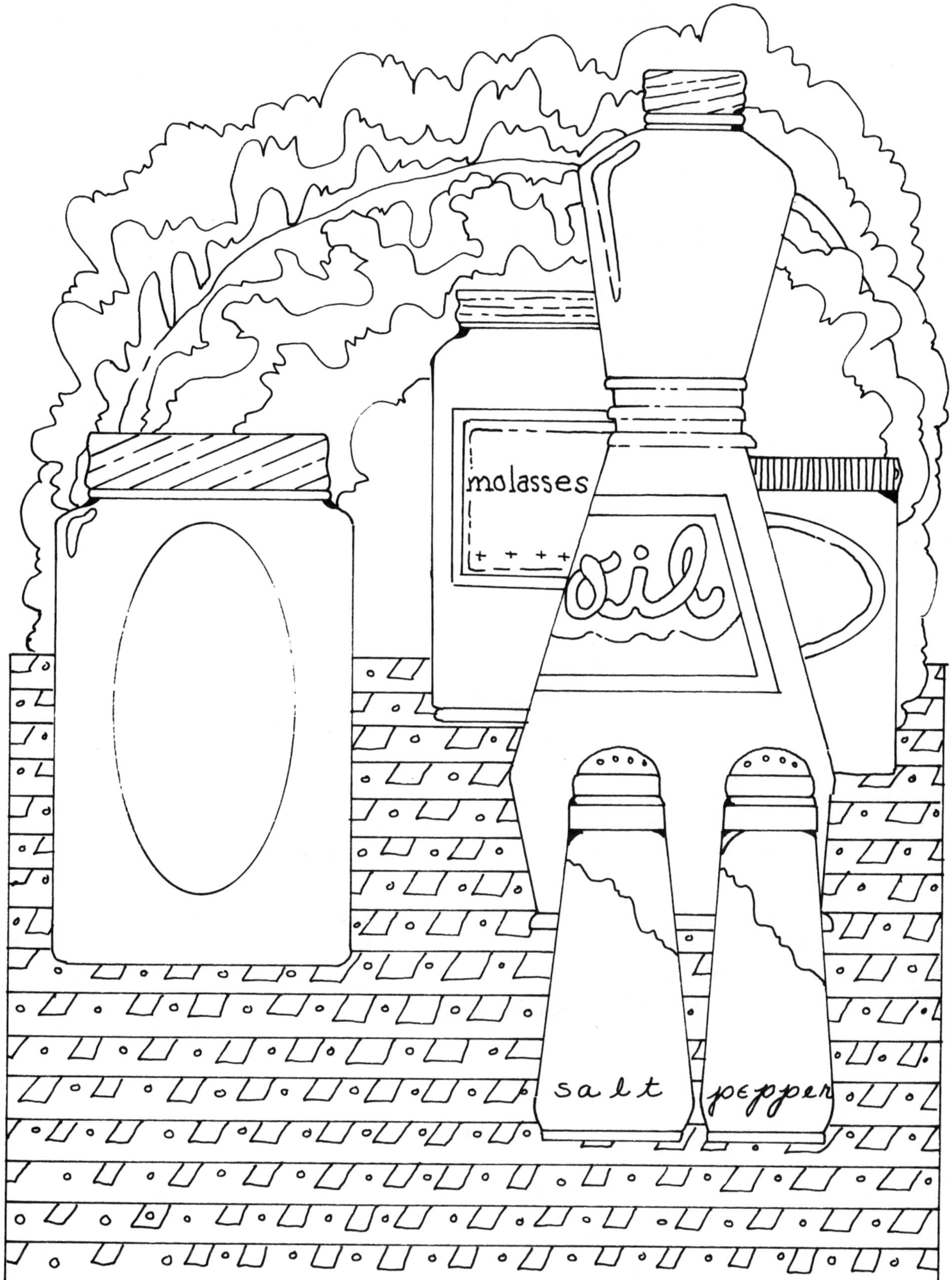
molasses
oil
salt
pepper

Orange-Honey Fruit Dressing

1 1/2 cup creamed cottage cheese
1/2 cup orange juice
1/2 cup honey
1/2 teaspoon ginger

Place cottage cheese in deep mixing bowl. Beat at medium speed. Slowly add orange juice, honey, and ginger. Beat dressing until smooth. Chill before serving.
  Makes 2 1/2 cups.
  Serve on fruit salad.

Oriental Dressing

1 tablespoon lemon juice
1 teaspoon grated lemon peel
1/2 teaspoon soy sauce
1/2 teaspoon prepared mustard
1 teaspoon rice vinegar
1 tablespoon salad oil

Combine all ingredients into a blender and blend. Chill before serving.
  Makes 1/4 cup.
  Serve with fresh vegetable salad.

Parmesan Dressing Rosé

1 egg
3/4 cup salad oil
1/2 cup rosé wine
3 tablespoons Parmesan cheese, grated

3 tablespoons wine vinegar
1/4 teaspoon seasoned salt
1/4 teaspoon paprika
1/2 clove garlic

Put all ingredients in blender. Blend until garlic is liquefied.
Makes 1 1/2 cups.
Serve with vegetables or tossed salad greens.

Peppered Avocado Dressing

1 cup mayonnaise
1 ripe avocado, peeled, seeded, cubed
1/3 cup lemon juice
2 tablespoons milk

1 tablespoon honey
1 teaspoon salt
1/4 teaspoon hot pepper sauce
1/2 clove garlic

Place all ingredients in blender. Blend until garlic clove is liquefied. Chill before serving.
Makes 2 cups.
Serve with tossed salad greens.

Pickled Beet Sour Cream Dressing

1 cup sour cream
2 tablespoons pickled beet juice
1 tablespoon prepared mustard
1/2 teaspoon salt

1 cup pickled beets, drained
1/4 cup parsley clusters
1/4 teaspoon ground allspice

Put all ingredients in blender. Blend until smooth. Chill before serving.
    Makes about 2 cups.
    Serve with a vegetable salad.

Annie's Tips
Dressings will store well, refrigerated in tightly-covered jar.

Pineapple Salad Dressing

1/2 cup mayonnaise
2 tablespoons lemon juice

1/2 cup flaked coconut
1 cup pineapple yogurt

Combine mayonnaise and lemon juice. Add coconut to mayonnaise mixture. Fold in yogurt. Chill before serving.
   Makes 2 cups.
   Serve on fruit salad and molded salad.

Quick Potato Salad Dressing

1/4 cup heavy cream
3 tablespoons white wine vinegar
2 tablespoons horseradish
2 teaspoons onion, grated
1 teaspoon salt
1/8 teaspoon white pepper
1/2 cup olive oil

Combine all ingredients except olive oil in screw-top jar. Cover and shake thoroughly. Add olive oil and again cover and shake.
    Makes about 1 cup.
    Serve over warm potato salad.

Sour Cream Slaw Dressing

1 cup diary sour cream
1/4 cup vinegar
3 tablespoons sugar
1 1/2 teaspoons salt
1 teaspoon celery seed

Blend all ingredients in blender or electric mixer.
    Makes about 1 1/4 cups.

Special Yogurt Dressing

1/2 cup yogurt
1 cup mayonnaise
1/4 small onion, minced
1 teaspoon Worcestershire sauce
1/8 teaspoon garlic powder
4 ounces Roquefort or blue
    cheese, crumbled

Mix all ingrdients with electric mixer. Chill before serving.
    Makes 2 cups.
    Serve with any vegetable salad.

Strawberry Dressing

1 1/2 cups sour cream
1 tablespoon strawberry gelatin
1 teaspoon lemon juice
1 cup strawberries, chopped

Combine sour cream, gelatin, and lemon juice. Stir strawberries into sour cream mixture. Chill before serving.
   Makes 2 1/2 cups.
   Serve with fruit salad.

Sweet Yogurt Dressing

1/2 cup yogurt
4 tablespoons honey
2 tablespoons lemon juice
1/8 teaspoon cinnamon

Mix all ingredients together by hand. Chill well before serving.
   Makes about 1/4 cup.
   Serve with mixed salad greens or vegetable salad.

Tangy Tomato Dressing

one 8-ounce can tomato sauce
2 tablespoons vinegar
1 tablespoon Worcestershire sauce
1 teaspoon sugar
1 teaspoon grated onion
1 teaspoon horseradish
1/2 teaspoon salt
1/4 teaspoon pepper
1 or 2 dashes hot pepper sauce

In screw-top jar, combine all ingredients. Cover and shake.
   Makes 1 cup.
   Serve with salad greens or vegetable salad.

Annie's Tips

Save used mayonnaise jars for dressing storage. The wide-mouth jar is most convenient for this purpose.

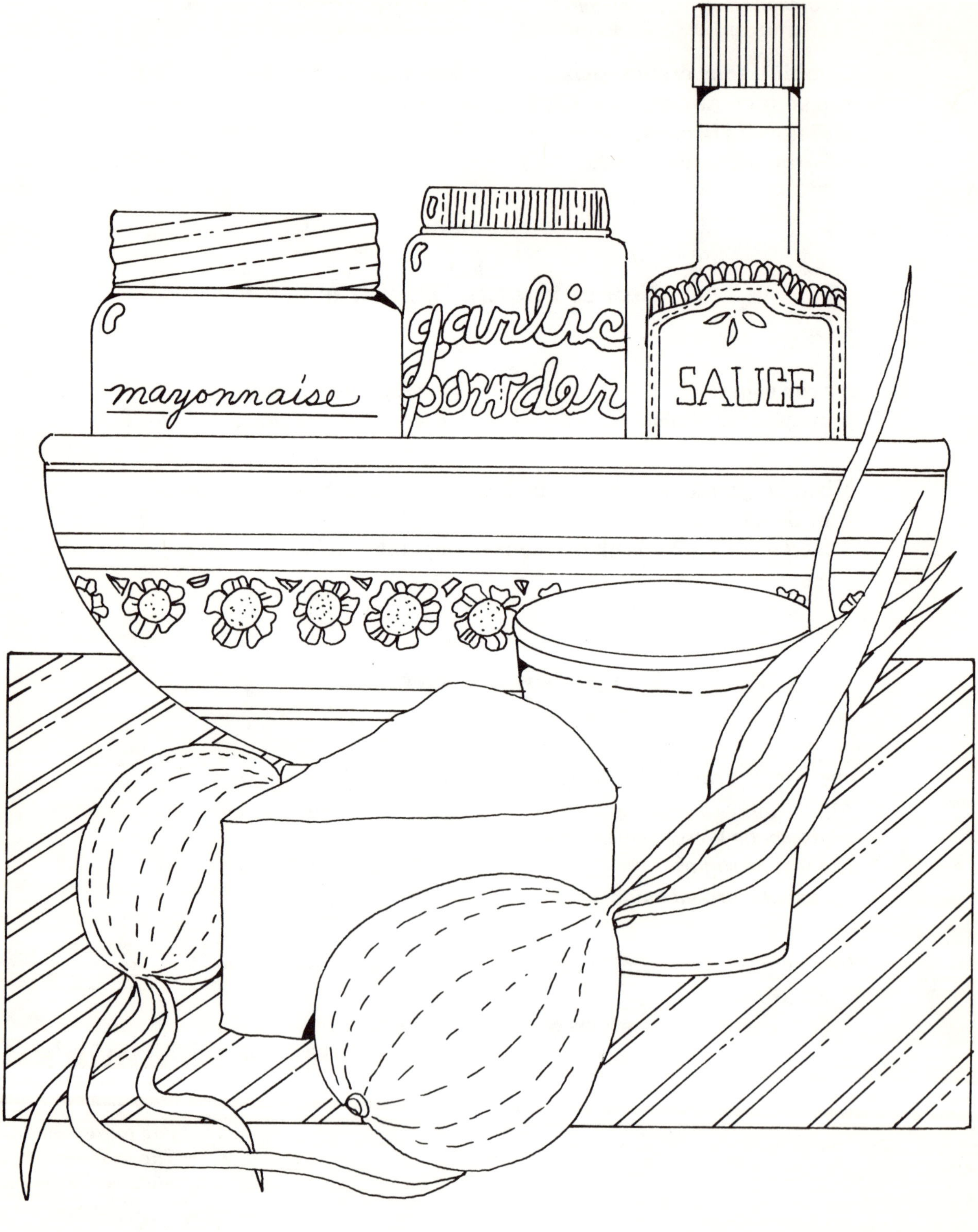
mayonnaise
garlic powder
SAUCE

Tarragon Sour Cream Dressing

1 1/2 teaspoons tarragon, crumbled
4 teaspoons white wine vinegar
1 1/2 cups sour cream

1 teaspoon sugar
3/4 teaspoon salt
1/4 teaspoon white pepper

Soak tarragon in vinegar for at least 1 hour. Add sugar, sour cream, salt, and white pepper to vinegar. Mix well. Chill before serving.

Makes about 1 1/2 cups.

Serve with fresh vegetable salad or seafood salad.

Tomato Honey Dressing

1 cup salad oil
1/2 cup catsup
1/3 cup vinegar
1/3 cup honey

1 teaspoon salt
1 teaspoon parprika
1 thin slice onion
1/4 clove garlic

Put all ingredients in blender. Blend until onion slice and garlic are liquefied. Chill well before serving.
    Makes 2 1/2 cups.
    Serve with tossed salad greens or vegetable salad.

Two-Cheese Dressing

3/4 cup milk
one 8-ounce package cream cheese, cubed
one 4-ounce package blue cheese

1/2 teaspoon tarragon
1 teaspoon salt
1/4 teaspoon pepper
1/4 clove garlic

Put all ingredients in blender. Blend until smooth and garlic is liquefied. Chill well before serving.
    Makes about 2 cups.
    Serve with vegetable salad.

White Wine Dressing

1/2 cup light salad oil
1/2 cup dry white wine
2 tablespoons vinegar
1/2 teaspoon sugar
1/2 teaspoon salt
1/2 teaspoon dried basil, crushed

Combine all ingredients in screw-top jar. Cover and shake well. Chill before serving.
    Makes about 1 cup.
    Serve with mixed vegetable salad or use as marinade for fresh vegetables.

Wine Dressing

6 tablespoons white wine vinegar
3 tablespoons medium dry sherry
1 tablespoon Worcestershire sauce
6 tablespoons olive oil
1/2 teaspoon seasoned salt
1/2 teaspoon salt
1/4 teaspoon pepper
2 tablespoons sugar
1 teaspoon paprika

Combine all ingredients in screw-top jar. Cover and shake until well blended. Chill before serving.
    Makes 1 cup.
    Serve on mixed vegetable salad.

Yogurt Dressing Supreme

1/2 cup yogurt
1/4 cup lemon juice
1/2 cup creamed cottage cheese
1 teaspoon salt
1/2 teaspoon paprika
1/2 green pepper, seeded and minced

Blend all ingredients, except green pepper, in blender or electric mixer. Blend until smooth. Add green pepper and mix well by hand. Chill well before serving.
    Makes 1 cup.
    Serve with vegetable salad or with seafood.

Yogurt Slaw Dressing

2 eggs, beaten
3 tablespoons honey
1 teaspoon salt
1 cup yogurt
1/4 cup lemon juice
1 teaspoon celery seed

In the top of a double boiler, blend all ingredients into smooth paste. Cook until smooth and thick.
    Makes about 2 cups.
    Serve with a vegetable salad.

Zesty Blue Cheese Dressing

1 cup mayonnaise
4 ounces blue cheese, crumbled
1/4 cup dry white wine

1 tablespoon grated onion
4–5 drops hot pepper sauce

Mix all ingredients together with electric mixer. Chill before serving.

Makes about 1 2/3 cups.

Serve with vegetable or tossed salad.

BIG GREEN SALADS

Asparagus and Mushroom Salad

1/2 cup Fines Herbes Vinaigrette Dressing
1/2 pound fresh raw mushrooms, thinly sliced
1 pound asparagus, steamed, cut into 1-inch pieces
1 cup yogurt
2 hard-boiled eggs, chopped
1 tablespoon fresh chives, chopped

Combine Fines Herbes Vinaigrette Dressing with sliced mushrooms in mixing bowl. Cover and marinate mixture in refrigerator for at least 30 minutes. Steam asparagus until just tender, about 10 minutes.

Combine yogurt and asparagus. Gently fold asparagus mixutre into mushroom mixture. Transfer salad to large serving dish. Garnish with chopped eggs and serve.

Makes four-to-six servings.

Avocado Gazpacho Salad

1/4 cup Honey French Dressing
4 avocado halves, peeled and seeded
1/2 cup green pepper, chopped
1/2 cup cucumber, chopped
1/2 cup tomato, chopped
2 tablespoons green onion, chopped
lettuce leaves

Combine green pepper, cucumber, tomato, onion, and Honey French Dressing. Mix lightly. Fill avocado halves with vegetable mixture. Place lettuce leaves on 4 individual salad plates. Place avocado halves on plates. Chill well before serving.

Makes four servings.

Avocado Spinach Salad

3/4 cup Creamy Bacon Dressing
1 avocado, peeled, seeded,
  sliced in wedges
1 pound raw fresh spinach

1/4 pound fresh raw
  mushrooms, sliced
1 Bermuda onion, sliced thin
2 tablespoons sesame seed

Wash and pat dry spinach leaves. Remove stems and tear spinach leaves into bite-size pieces. Combine spinach with mushrooms, onion, and sesame seed. Arrange spinach mixture in salad bowl with avocado wedges. Top salad with Creamy Bacon Dressing.
   Makes four-to-six servings.

Annie's Tips
To refresh, plunge hot food into cold water to quickly stop the cooking process and avoid over-cooking.

Bean Sprout and Cucumber Salad

1/2 cup Ginger Dressing
1/2 pound fresh bean sprouts
2 cucumbers, cut lengthwise in
  1/4-inch slices; cut slices
  into 1/4-inch strips

1 tablespoon salt
1 small onion, sliced thin
1 tablespoon sesame seed
lettuce leaves

Put cucumber in bowl and sprinkle with salt. Let stand for 30 minutes. Put sprouts in collander and pour 1 quart boiling water over them. Refresh sprouts with cold water.
   Drain cucumber and sprouts, and place in clean dry bowl. Add onion and Ginger Dressing to mixture. Toss salad with sesame seed and chill for at least 1 hour. Divide salad into four individual lettuce-lined salad plates.
   Makes four servings.

Bean Sprout and Mushroom Salad

1/2 cup White Wine Dressing
1 medium onion, sliced thin
2 tablespoons butter
1/2 pound fresh raw
   mushrooms, sliced

1 pound fresh bean sprouts
1 tablespoon sesame seed
lettuce leaves

In a skillet sauté sliced onion in butter for 1 minute. Add mushrooms to skillet and sauté mixture until mushrooms are just wilted. Transfer mixture to bowl.

Put sprouts in collander and pour 1 quart boiling water over them. Drain sprouts and add to bowl containing mushroom mixture. Pour White Wine Dressing over vegetables in bowl and add sesame seed. Toss salad well and chill for at least 1 hour. Divide mixutre into 4 individual lettuce-lined salad plates.

Makes four servings.

Beet Salad

1 1/2 cups Beet Dressing
1 1/2 pounds fresh beets
1 small clove garlic, halved
1 head lettuce

1/4 cup green onion, sliced
one 7-ounce can tuna, chilled, drained, flaked
1/2 cup celery, sliced

Cut off all but 1 inch of stem and roots of fresh beets; do not pare. Cook, covered, in boiling salted water about 35 minutes or until tender. Drain, pare, and slice. Chill.

Just before serving, rub salad bowl with halved garlic. Combine lettuce and onion in salad bowl. Arrange beets, tuna, and celery atop salad greens. Toss salad gently with Beet Dressing. Garnish with additional sliced green onion, if desired.

Makes six-to-eight servings.

Annie's Tips

Wash and dry thoroughly all salad greens, fruits, and vegetables just before preparing salad. Never wash fruits or vegetables until ready to use.

Broccoli-Tomato Salad

1 cup Cheese and Lemon
   Dressing
1 bunch broccoli (1/2 pound)

3 medium tomatoes, cut in
   wedges
lettuce leaves

Wash broccoli thoroughly. Remove florets; use stalks another time. Cook florets in boiling salted water for 3 to 4 minutes; or use steamer. Drain well. Cool.

Pour 1 cup Cheese and Lemon Dressing over broccoli. Stir to coat. Chill 2 to 3 hours. Arrange broccoli and tomato wedges on bed of lettuce. Serve with additional dressing in side dish.

Makes five-to-six servings.

Buz's Mixed Seafood Salad

1 cup Dill Sour Cream Dressing
2 cups cooked mixed shellfish (crabmeat, lobster, shrimp), peeled and cleaned
1 small head iceberg lettuce, torn in bite-size pieces
1 cup red cabbage, shredded
1 cup carrot, grated
1/2 cup green pepper, diced
1 medium cucumber, pared and sliced
1/2 pound fresh raw mushrooms, sliced
1 teaspoon celery seed

Prepare shellfish and combine in bowl. Set aside. In large salad bowl combine lettuce, cabbage, carrots, green peppers, cucumbers, and mushrooms. Add prepared shellfish to salad mixture. Chill for at least 1 hour.

Pour Dill Sour Cream Dressing over salad. Add celery seed and toss.

Makes six-to-eight servings.

Cauliflower Salad

1/2 cup Tangy Tomato Dressing
1 small head cauliflower, separated into florets, chopped
6 radishes, chopped fine
1 small onion, chopped fine
lettuce leaves
chopped parsley

Combine cauliflower, onion, and radishes. Mix vegetables with Tangy Tomato Dressing and chill thoroughly. Line a deep salad bowl with lettuce leaves. Fill lined salad bowl with cauliflower salad and garnish with chopped parsley.

Makes four-to-six servings.

Celery Slaw

1 1/4 cups Sour Cream Slaw
 Dressing
1 bunch celery, separated into
 stalks, chopped
3 medium carrots, grated

1 medium onion, diced
lettuce leaves
1/4 cup bean sprouts

Combine celery, carrots, and onion in large mixing bowl. Add Sour Cream Slaw Dressing and combine mixture well. Chill for several hours.

Serve slaw in lettuce-lined salad bowl. Garnish with sprouts. Makes eight servings.

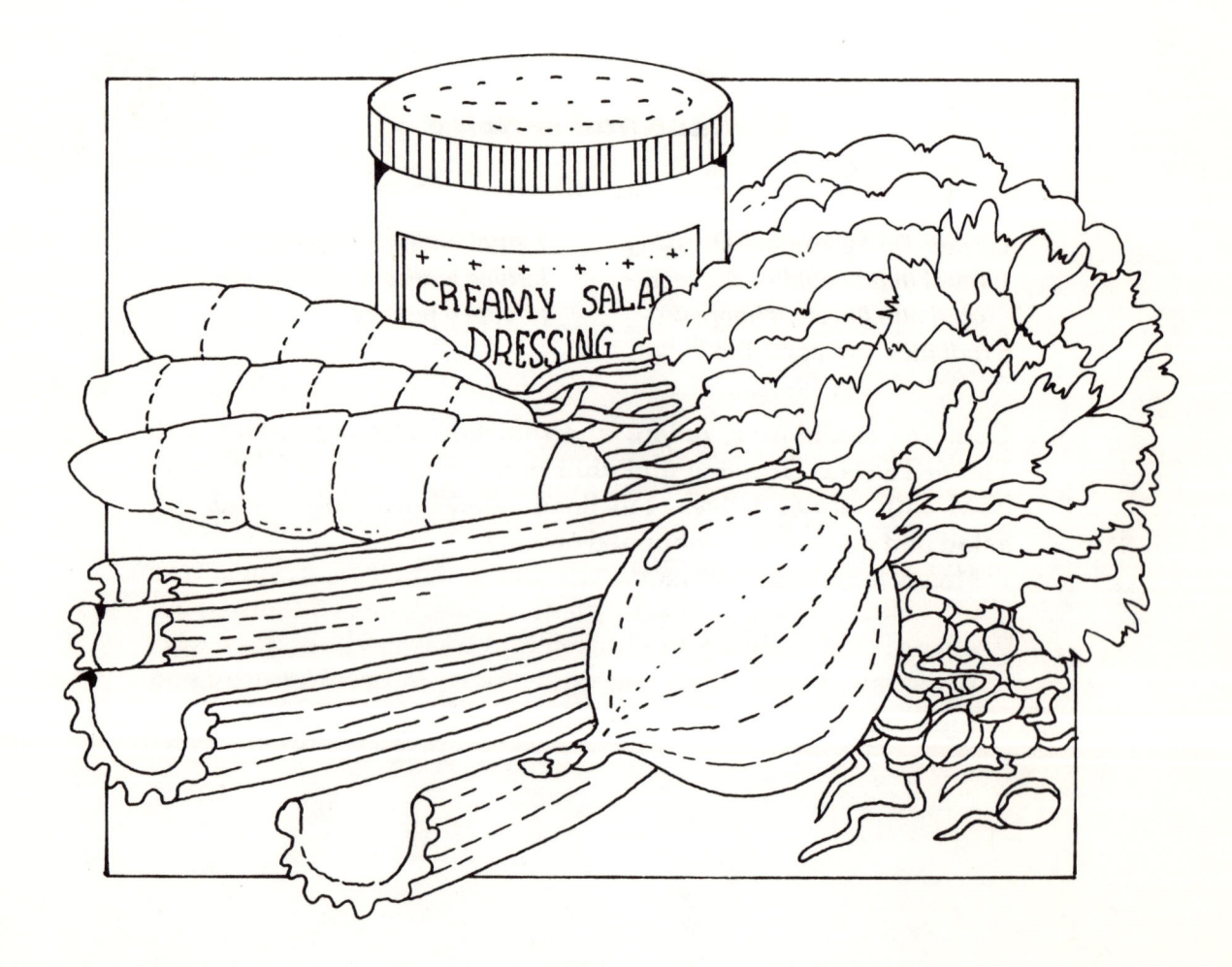

Cheese Spinach Salad

1 cup Ginger Dressing
1 pound raw fresh spinach
2 hard-boiled eggs, finely chopped
1/3 cup celery, finely chopped
1/3 cup onion, finely chopped
1/2 cup sharp cheese, cubed
1/2 cup mung bean sprouts

Wash and pat dry spinach leaves. Remove stems and tear spinach leaves into bite-size pieces. Combine spinach with eggs, celery, onion, cheese, and sprouts. Toss salad gently with Ginger Dressing. Serve with additional dressing in side dish.
   Makes four servings.

Annie's Tips
Wrap vegetables in plastic wrap and keep refrigerated until ready to use.

Chicken and Ham Salad

1 1/2 cups Creamy Salad Dressing
2 cups cooked chicken, diced
1 1/2 cups cooked ham, cut into 1/2-inch cubes
2 cups celery, diced
1 cup apple, peeled, cored, diced
1 carrot, cut into thin strips
1 large tomato, diced
1/2 cup seedless green grapes, halved
1/2 cup pitted ripe olives, sliced
1 tablespoon parsley, finely snipped
1/2 teaspoon dried rosemary, crushed

Combine chicken, ham, celery, apples, tomatoes, grapes, and olives in large bowl. Stir parsley and rosemary into Creamy Salad Dressing. Add dressing to chicken and ham mixture. Toss mixture to coat. Cover bowl and chill. Serve in deep lettuce-lined salad bowl. Garnish with thin carrot strips.
   Makes eight servings.

Crab Salad

1/2 cup Dill Sour Cream Dressing
1 small head lettuce, shredded
1 pound backfin crabmeat
4 scallions, finely chopped
1/4 pound raw fresh
  mushrooms, sliced

3 hard-boiled eggs,
  cut into wedges
3 medium ripe tomatoes,
  cut into wedges
1/2 cup black pitted olives

Combine crabmeat with scallions and mushrooms. Add 1/2 cup Dill Sour Cream Dressing. Arrange crabmeat mixture in mound on shredded lettuce. Arrange eggs, tomatoes, and olives around the salad. Serve with additional dressing in side dish.
   Makes four servings.

Cucumber-Radish Salad

1 cup Lemon-Cucumber
  Dressing
1 tablespoon salt
3 medium cucumbers, pared

1 onion, sliced thin
6 radishes, sliced thin
lettuce leaves
2 tablespoons chopped walnuts

Halve cucumbers lengthwise and slice. Put cucumbers in bowl and sprinkle with salt. Let stand for 30 minutes. Drain cucumbers and squeeze out excess moisture. Put cucumbers in clean dry bowl. Add onion and radishes. Add Lemon-Cucumber Dressing and mix well. Chill for at least 3 hours.

Transfer mixture to lettuce-lined salad bowl and garnish with walnuts.

Makes four servings.

Cucumber and Shrimp Salad

1/2 cup Dill Sour Cream Dressing
3 large cucumbers, pared
1 tablespoon salt

1 cup tiny shrimp, cooked,
  peeled, and cleaned
lettuce leaves

Prepare shrimp. Refrigerate in covered bowl. Halve cucumbers lengthwise and slice very thin. Put cucumbers in bowl and sprinkle with salt. Let stand for 30 minutes.

Drain cucumbers and squeeze out excess moisture. Put cucumbers in clean dry bowl. Add Dill Sour Cream Dressing. Cover bowl and chill for least 2 hours. Stir shrimp into cucumber mixture just before serving. Serve in lettuce-lined salad bowl.

Makes four servings.

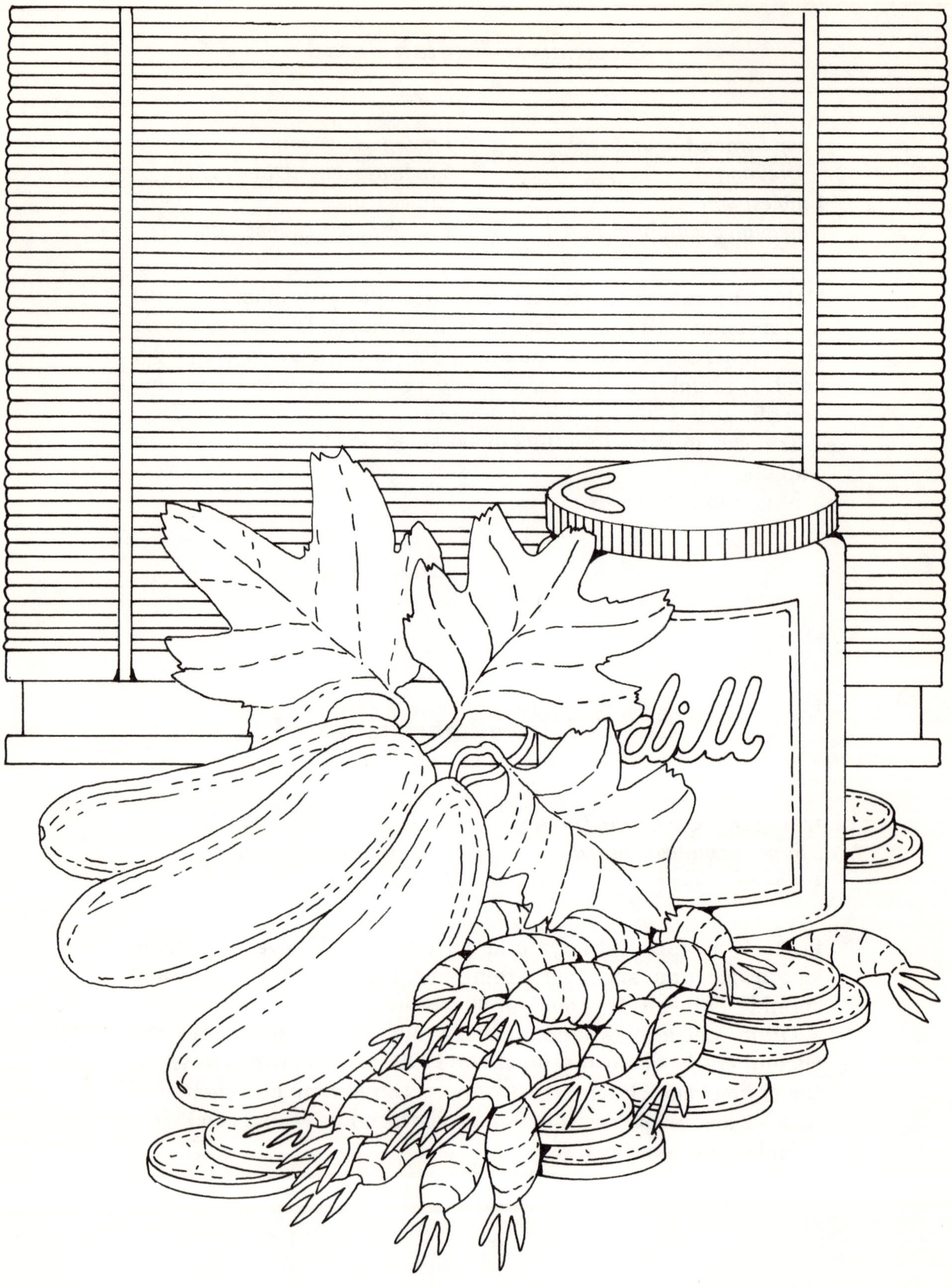
dill

Gazpacho Salad

1 recipe Avocado Dressing
4 medium tomatoes, sliced thin
1 cucumber, sliced thin
1 small Spanish onion, sliced thin
4 radishes, sliced thin
1/2 cup sprouts
1/4 pound fresh raw mushrooms, sliced thin
2 cups red cabbage, shredded
2 tablespoons minced parsley
1/2 cup croutons

In a glass bowl arrange layers of tomatoes, cucumber, onion, radishes, mushrooms, and cabbage. Pour Avocado Dressing over vegetables. Cover bowl and chill for 4 hours.

Just before serving, garnish salad with sprouts, parsley, and croutons.

Makes four servings.

Green Salad with Hard-Boiled Egg

1 cup Herbed Sour Cream Dressing
1 head Boston lettuce, torn in bite-size pieces
3 hard-boiled eggs, sliced
1/4 cup scallion, minced
1 hard-boiled egg, chopped
paprika

Combine Boston lettuce, sliced eggs, and scallions in salad bowl. Add Herbed Sour Cream Dressing and toss salad. Garnish with chopped egg and sprinkle salad with paprika.

Makes four servings.

Annie's Tips
Storage: Washing before storage will promote decay.

Japanese Salad

1/4 cup Oriental Dressing
2 small carrots, cut in strips
1 small zucchini, cut in strips
1 cucumber, cut in strips
1/2 cup bean sprouts
1/2 cup celery, diced
1/2 cup fresh raw mushrooms, sliced
1/2 cup watercress
lettuce leaves

Combine all vegetables except lettuce in bowl. Add Oriental Dressing to vegetables and toss well. Serve in lettuce-lined salad bowl.
    Makes four servings.

Annie's Tips
Keep vegetables cold and crisp unless recipe indicates otherwise.

Marinated Avocado-Mushroom Salad

1/2 cup White Wine Dressing
1 medium avocado, seeded, peeled, and sliced
lettuce leaves
1 cup fresh raw mushrooms, sliced
2 medium onions, sliced thin

Combine avocado and mushrooms in bowl. Separate onions into rings and add to avocado mixture. Pour White Wine Dressing over vegetables. Cover bowl and marinate in refrigerator for about 3 hours.
    Drain avocado mixture. Spoon mixture into lettuce-lined salad plate.
    Makes four servings.

Marinated Zucchini with Tomato Salad

1 cup Yogurt Dressing Supreme
1 pound zucchini, thinly sliced
  (2 cups)

2 medium tomatoes, sliced
lettuce leaves

Steam zucchini until tender-crisp, about 2 to 3 minutes. Drain well. Add Yogurt Dressing Supreme to zucchini. Toss to coat. Chill for about 2 to 3 hours.

Arrange tomato slices on lettuce leaves on platter. Top platter with marinated zucchini.

Makes four-to-five servings.

Mixed Salad

1 scant cup French Mustard Dressing
1 medium cucumber, pared
1 avocado, peeled, pitted, and sliced
2 large bananas, sliced
lettuce leaves
1 large green pepper, seeded, cut in thin strips
1 mild red pepper, seeded, cut in thin strips
1/2 small onion, very thinly sliced and separated into rings

Halve cucumber lengthwise; remove seeds and slice crosswise. Combine cucumber with avocado, bananas, peppers, and onion in salad bowl. Pour French Mustard Dressing over mixture. Cover salad bowl and marinate in refrigerator for about 2 hours.
   Toss mixture gently and serve in lettuce-lined bowl.
   Makes six servings.

Mushroom and Bacon Salad

1 cup White Wine Dressing
1/4 teaspoon freshly ground black pepper
1 pound fresh raw mushrooms, sliced thin
6 strips bacon, cooked crisp, drained, crumbled
2 celery stalks, trimmed, finely chopped
1 tablespoon fresh parsley, chopped
1 tablespoon fresh chives, chopped
lettuce leaves

Combine White Wine Dressing, black pepper, and mushrooms in mixing bowl. Cover bowl and chill for about 30 minutes. Arrange lettuce leaves on individual salad plates.
   Use slotted spoon to transfer mushrooms onto lettuce leaves. Reserve dressing to serve over salad. Add celery, bacon, parsley, and chives to each salad plate. Serve immediately with reserved dressing in sauce dish.
   Makes six servings.

Sesame Lettuce Salad

1 1/2 cups French-Style Blue Cheese Dressing
2 tablespoons sesame seed
1 small head lettuce
1/2 cup green pepper, chopped
2 green onions, sliced
one 11-ounce can mandarin orange sections, drained
1/2 medium cucumber, sliced

In skillet toast sesame seed till lightly browned. Add sesame seed to French-Style Blue Cheese Dressing. Combine lettuce, green pepper, and onions. Arrange lettuce mixture, orange sections, and cucumber in salad bowl. Pour salad dressing atop, toss lightly, and serve.
    Makes four-to-six servings.

Annie's Tips

Preparation: When preparing salads, keep them simple, neat ,and interesting.

Special Green Salad

2 1/2 cups Tomato Honey
    Dressing
1 small head iceberg lettuce
1/2 pound fresh spinach
1 cup curly escarole
1 medium cucumber, sliced thin
1/2 pound raw fresh mushrooms
1 Bermuda onion, sliced
1/2 cup alfalfa or mung-bean
    sprouts

Wash lettuce, spinach, and escarole. Pat dry and tear into bite-size pieces. Place greens in salad bowl. Add cucumber, mushrooms, onion, and sprouts to salad greens. Toss salad gently with 1 cup Tomato Honey Dressing. Serve with additional dressing in a side dish.
    Makes four-to-six servings.

Special Tossed Romaine

1 cup Parmesan Dressing Rosé
6 strips bacon, cooked crisp,
    drained, crumbled
2 heads romaine, torn in
    bite-size pieces
2 cups cherry tomatoes, halved
1 cup croutons
1 cup Swiss cheese,
    coarsely grated
2/3 cup slivered almonds,
    toasted
1/3 cup Parmesan cheese,
    grated

Combine bacon, romaine, tomatoes, Swiss cheese, almonds, and Parmesan cheese in large salad bowl. Toss salad with Parmesan Dressing Rosé. Add salt and pepper to taste. Garnish with croutons.
    Makes eight servings.

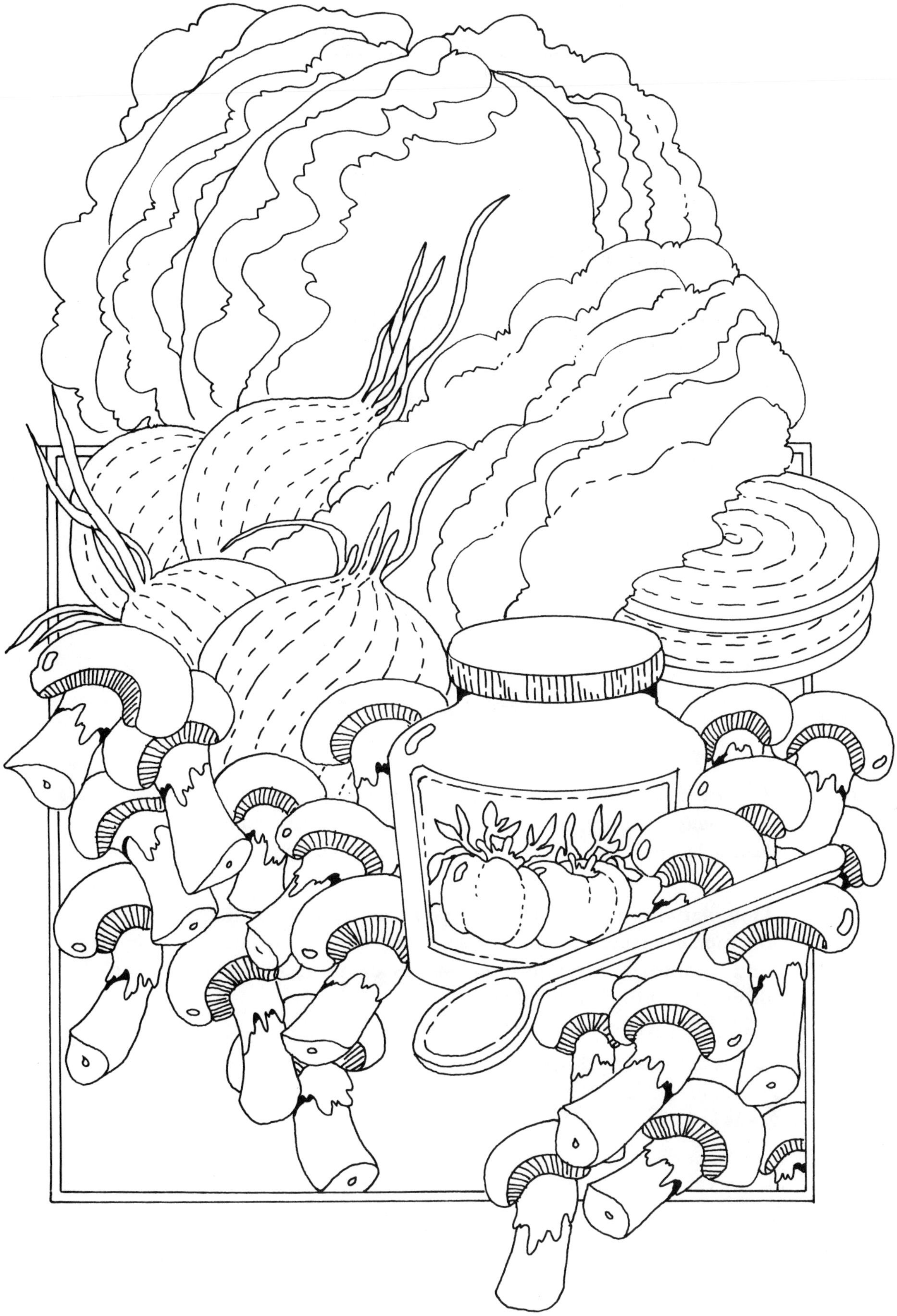

Sweet Pepper Salad

1 cup Wine Dressing
4 green peppers
4 red peppers

16 pitted black olives
8 ounces cream cheese,
   cut into cubes

Wash peppers and cut into halves. Remove seeds and white pith. Cut each half into quarters. Steam peppers for 3 minutes. Remove from steamer and let cool on paper towel. Combine peppers with Wine Dressing in mixing bowl. Cover and marinate in refrigerator for about 24 hours.

To serve, place marinated peppers in shallow bowl. Arrange olives and cream cheese atop peppers. Spoon a little marinade over salad.

Makes four-to-six servings.

Tomato-Beef Salad

1 2/3 cups Horseradish Dressing
3 medium tomatoes, sliced
lettuce leaves

1 pound cold roast beef, sliced
2 small green onions,
   sliced in rings

Line platter with lettuce. Arrange slices of roast beef and tomato on top of lettuce. Pour 2/3 cup Horseradish Dressing over beef and tomatoes. Arrange onion slices on platter. Serve with additional dressing in side dish.

Makes three-to-four servings.

Annie's Tips
It has been said by many that we eat with our eyes.

Tomato Salad Rosé

1 1/2 cups Parmesan Dressing Rosé
4 large tomatoes, peeled and thinly sliced
1/2 cup celery, finely chopped
1 small onion, sliced thin
lettuce leaves

Place tomatoes, celery, and onion in shallow dish or deep bowl. Pour Parmesan Dressing Rosé over tomato mixture. Cover and chill for several hours.

Lift tomato mixture from dressing and spread onto lettuce leaves. Spoon some dressing over tomatoes. Serve with additional dressing in side dish.

Makes four-to-six servings.

Annie's Tips
Serve salads in chilled bowl or salad plate.

Tomatoes Stuffed with Beets

1 1/2 cups Tarragon Sour Cream Dressing
3 1/2 cups cooked or canned beets, drained and minced
4 large firm tomatoes
salt
lettuce leaves
fresh tarragon, minced
snipped parsley

Cut tops off tomatoes. Use grapefruit knife to remove seeds and pulp. Sprinkle insides of each tomato with salt, and invert on paper towel to drain for at least 30 minutes.

In bowl combine beets with Tarragon Sour Cream Dressing. Fill tomato shells with beet mixture. Chill stuffed tomatoes for at least 1 hour.

Serve each tomato on lettuce-lined salad plate. Garnish with minced fresh tarragon and snipped parsley.

Makes four servings.

Tomatoes Stuffed with Shrimp Salad

1/2 cup Dill Sour Cream Dressing
6 large firm tomatoes
3/4 teaspoon salt
1 medium cucumber, peeled, seeded, and chopped
1 pound small shrimps, peeled and chopped
lettuce leaves
6 fresh dill sprigs

Put cucumbers in bowl and sprinkle with 3/4 teaspoon salt. Let stand for 30 minutes. Drain. Cut tops off tomatoes. Use grapefruit knife to remove seeds and pulp. Chop pulp and drain in sieve. Sprinkle insides of each tomato with salt and invert on paper towel to drain for at least 30 minutes.

Reserve 6 shrimps from pound for garnish. Chop remaining shrimp coarsely and place in mixing bowl. Add drained cucumbers and tomato pulp to shrimps. Add Dill Sour Cream Dressing and mix well. Chill.

Fill tomato shells with shrimp mixture. Place each stuffed tomato on lettuce-lined salad plate. Garnish top of each stuffed tomato with a whole shrimp and sprig of dill.

Makes six servings.

Tuna Salad in Pepper Cups

3/4 cup Creamy Bacon Dressing
5 medium green peppers, halved lengthwise, seeded
2 medium carrots, grated
2 stalks celery, chopped
lettuce leaves
2 tablespoons chopped onion
one 7-ounce can tuna, drained and flaked
1 medium firm tomato, sliced very thin
snipped parsley

Substitute honey with 1 tablespoon prepared mustard when preparing Creamy Bacon Dressing. Steam peppers for 5 minutes. Drain and chill.

Combine carrots, celery, onion, and tuna in mixing bowl. Pour Creamy Bacon Dressing over tuna mixture and toss lightly. Chill. Sprinkle inside of peppers with salt. Fill peppers with tuna mixture.

Serve stuffed peppers on lettuce-lined plates. Garnish top of each pepper with sliced tomato and parsley.

Makes five servings.

Vegetable Salad Plate with Dip

2 cups Two-Cheese Dressing
1 small bunch celery, separated into stalks
1/2 pound string beans, snap ends
1 green pepper, seeded and sliced
1 head cauliflower, separated into florets
2 small cucumbers, peeled, cut into quarters lengthwise
1 bunch radishes, sliced thick
1/2 pound fresh raw mushrooms, sliced thick
1 pint cherry tomatoes
olives stuffed with pimento
parsley

Place saucedish in center of large round platter. Arrange prepared vegetables on platter to look like pie wedges. Fill saucedish with Two-Cheese Dressing. Garnish salad plate with olives and parsley.

Serve as hors d'oeuvre.

Annie's Tips

Use fresh flowers from your garden to enhance the appearance of your salads. Many flowers are edible, but it is best to consider them a decorative garnish.

Vegetable-Shrimp Salad

3/4 cup Tarragon Sour Cream Dressing
1 pound cooked shrimp, peeled and cleaned
3 large carrots, grated
1 1/2 cups small green beans, snap ends, cut lengthwise
1/2 pound fresh raw mushrooms, sliced thin
lettuce leaves

Prepare shrimp. Refrigerate in covered bowl. Combine carrots, green beans, and mushrooms in bowl. Add shrimp and Tarragon Sour Cream Dressing. Toss salad lightly. Serve in lettuce-lined salad bowl.

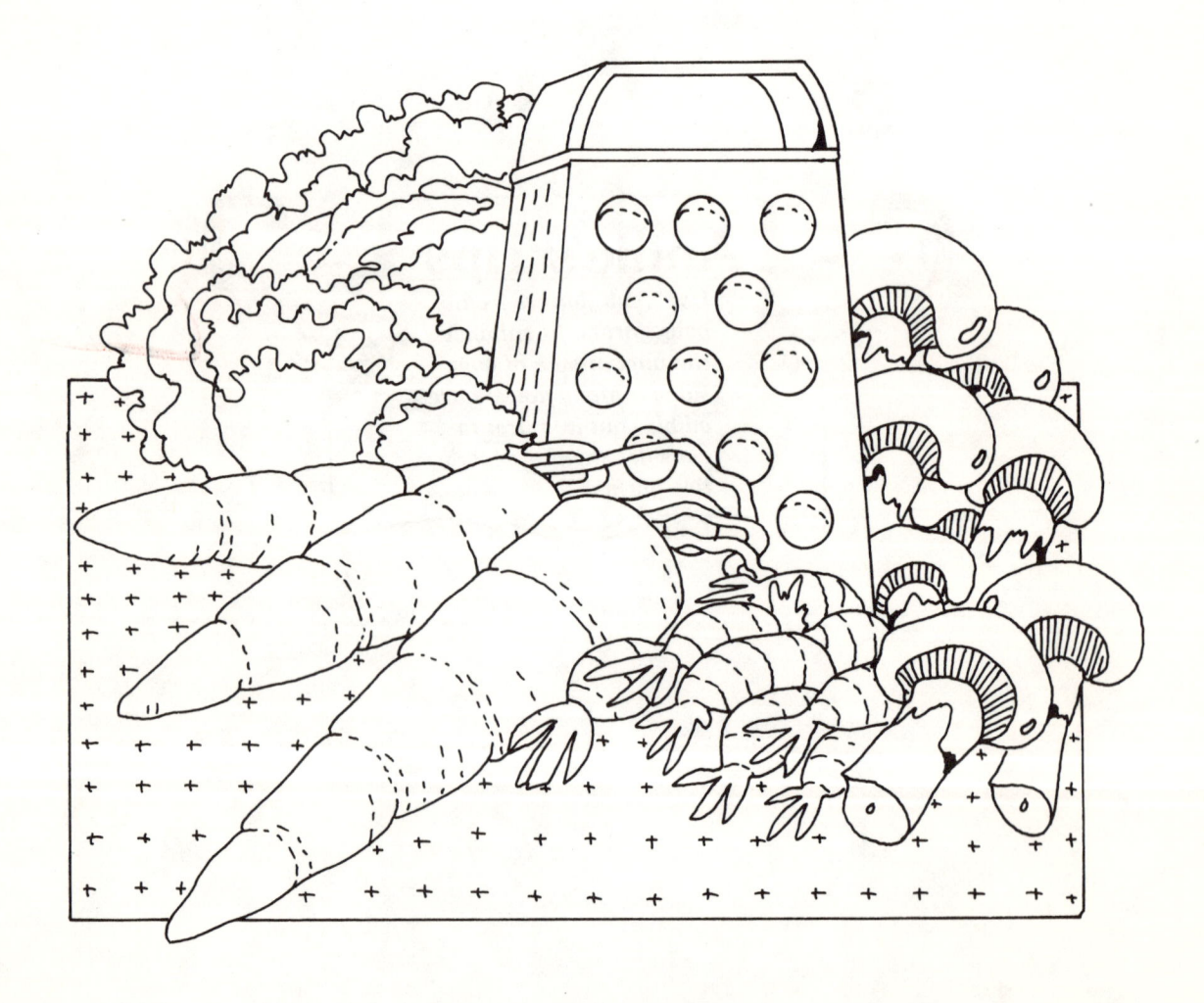

Makes four servings.

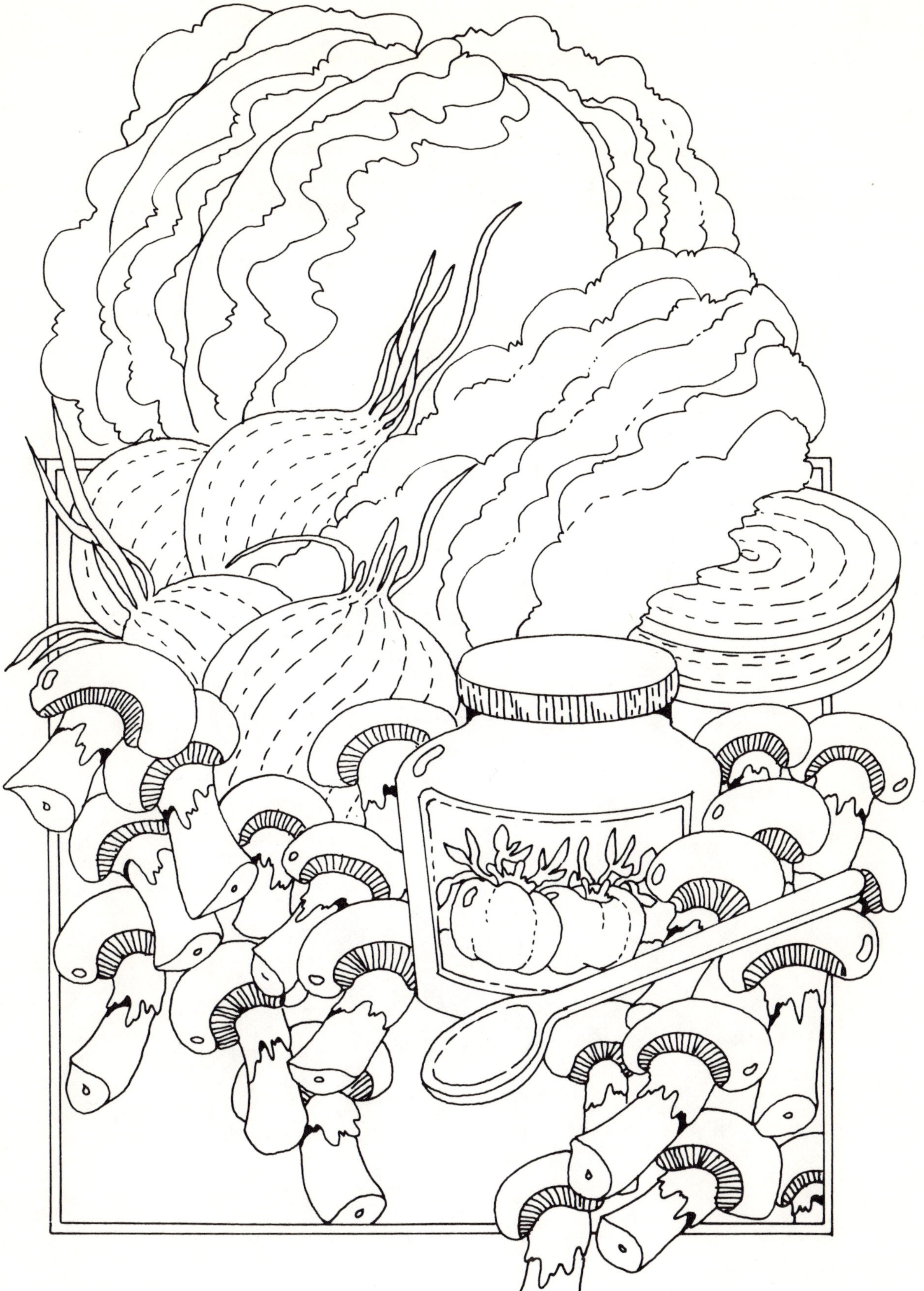

FRUIT SALADS

Apple-Raisin Slaw

1 cup Lemon Dressing
1 cup golden raisins
1 cup rosé wine
1 tablespoon lemon juice
3 apples, cored and diced
4 cups cabbage, shredded

Combine raisins and wine. Cover and let stand for several hours. Sprinkle lemon juice over apples. Add raisin-and-wine mixture to apples. Combine mixture with cabbage. Toss with Lemon Dressing. Chill before serving.
    Makes six servings.

Bananas and Pears with Port

3 pears, peeled, cored, sliced
2 bananas, sliced
1/4 cup golden raisins
1/4 cup sliced almonds
1/2 cup sweet Port wine
1/4 cup orange juice
2 tablespoons lemon juice
lettuce leaves

Combine pears, bananas, raisins, and almonds in bowl. Add Port, orange juice, and lemon juice. Toss mixture lightly. Cover and chill for at least 3 hours. Serve in lettuce-lined salad cups.
    Makes four servings

Banana Split Salad

1 cup Mocha Dressing
endive
4 bananas

1 pint strawberries
1/2 cup coconut
1 cup blueberries

Line 4 banana-split dishes with endive. Peel bananas and slice in half lengthwise. Place sliced banana atop each lined dish. Reserve four large strawberries for garnish. Hull and slice remaining strawberries. Combine sliced strawberries, blueberries, and coconut. Divide mixture between the four dishes. Spoon about 1/4 cup Mocha Dressing atop each salad. Garnish each dish with whole strawberry.

Makes four servings.

Beet Fruit Salad

3 tablespoons red wine vinegar
1 teaspoon tarragon, crumbled
1/2 cup sugar
3 beets, cooked, peeled, chopped, salted
lettuce leaves

3 naval oranges, peeled, sectioned
3 bananas, sliced
3 tart apples, cored, sliced
1/3 cup walnuts, chopped

Combine tarragon, sugar, and vinegar in bowl. Add beets and onion. Add oranges, bananas, and apples. Cover bowl and chill for at least 2 hours. Serve on lettuce-lined chilled platter. Garnish with walnuts.

Makes eight servings.

Annie's Tips

Do not wash fruit until ready to use. Washing fruit before use will promote decay.

Cheese and Fruit Salad

1/2 pint cottage cheese
1/2 pound Danish blue cheese
1/2 cup sour cream
lettuce leaves
apple wedges

fresh pears, sliced
white seedless grapes
strawberries
mint leaves

Beat cheese and sour cream until well blended. Arrange cheese mixture in center of plate lined with lettuce leaves. Chill. Arrange prepared fresh fruit around cheese. Decorate top of cheese with mint leaves.

Makes eight-to-ten servings.

Citrus Salad

1 1/2 cups Citrus Dressing
6 oranges, peeled, seeded, sectioned
lettuce leaves
2 avocados, peeled, seeded, sliced
3 grapefruits, peeled, seeded, sectioned

Line individual salad plates with lettuce leaves. Arrange orange sections, grapefruit sections, and avocado slices on each plate. Spoon Citrus Dressing over each salad. Serve with additional dressing on table.
    Makes six servings.

Cream Cheese Fruit Salad

3/4 cup Cream Cheese Dressing
1 1/2 cups red grapes, split and seeded
1 large red apple, cored and diced
1 1/2 cups mandarin oranges, drained
1/4 cup slivered almonds
lettuce leaves

Combine grapes, diced apples, oranges, and almonds. Toss mixture with Cream Cheese Dressing. Serve on lettuce-lined salad plates.
    Makes four servings.

Annie's Tips

Refrigerate ripened fruit that you are not using to retard spoilage.

Fruit Salad Platter

1 recipe Fresh Fruit Dressing
3 grapefruits
6 oranges, peeled and sectioned
1 can pineapple spears, drained
3 tangerines
2 cups cream-style cottage cheese
romaine leaves

Line platter with romaine. Put cottage cheese in small glass bowl and place on platter. Arrange fruits atop romaine. Serve Fresh Fruit Dressing in separate dish and spoon over fruit salad platter.
    Makes eight servings.

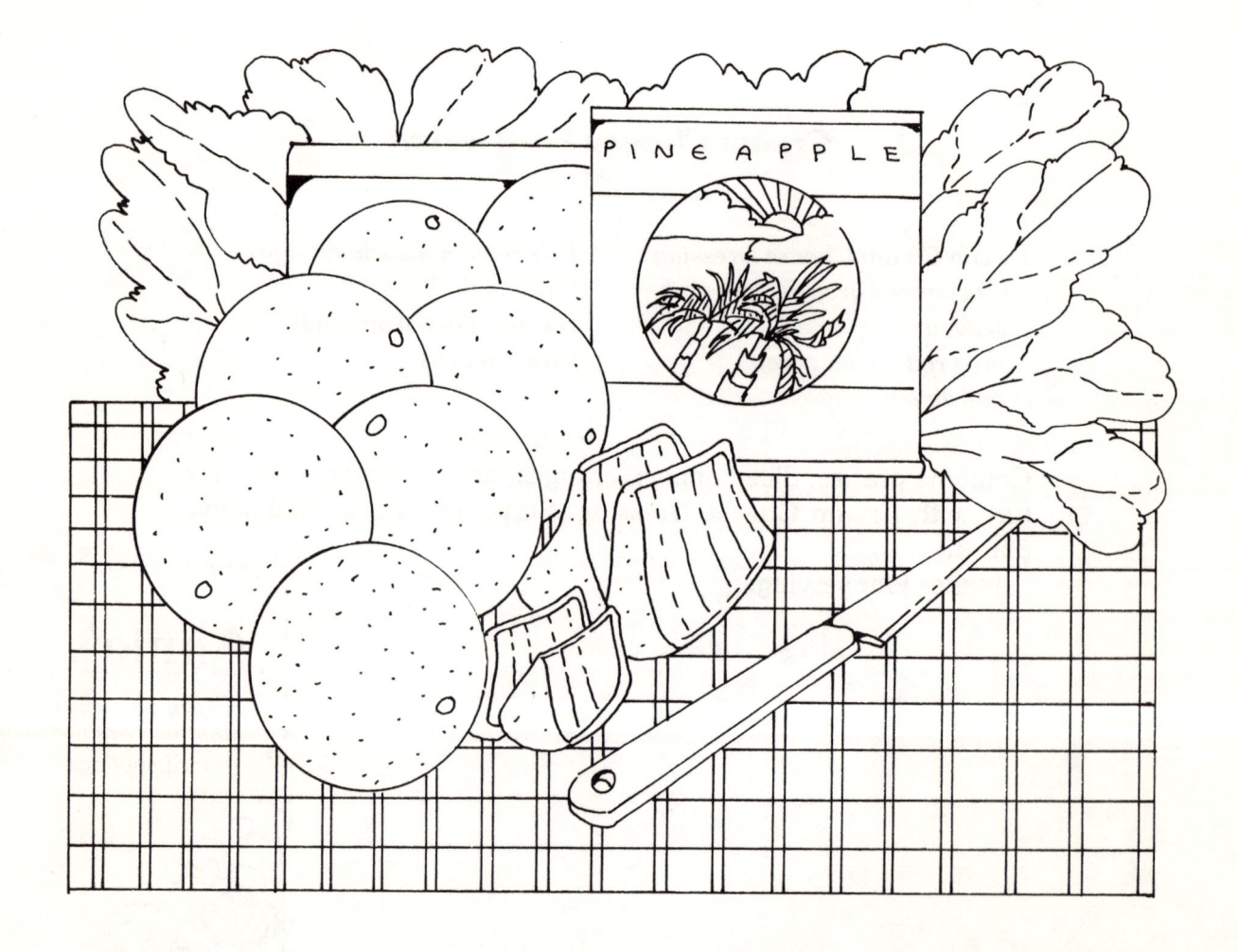

Fruit Salad with Shrimp

1/2 cup Dill Sour Cream Dressing
1 1/2 pounds cooked tiny shrimp
2 tablespoons lemon juice
2 tablespoons lime juice
4 ounces shredded coconut
2 bananas, thinly sliced

4-ounce can chunky pineapple, drained
4 medium tomatoes, cut in quarters, seeded, diced
1 red pepper, seeded, chopped
1 green pepper, seeded, chopped

Combine shrimps in mixing bowl with lemon juice and lime juice. Toss mixture, cover, and refrigerate. In large mixing bowl combine coconut, bananas, pineapple, tomatoes, red pepper, and green pepper. Toss mixture with 1/2 cup Dill Sour Cream Dressing. Add shrimps and toss again. Cover bowl and chill for at least 1 hour before serving.

Makes six servings.

Annie's Tips

Remove the white membrane, called pith, from citrus fruit after peeling. The pith has a bitter taste.

Ginger Summer Salad

1/2 cup blueberries
1 cup honeydew balls
1 cup cantaloupe balls
1 cup watermelon balls
1 pint strawberries, hulled, halved if large

2 small bananas, sliced
1 cup seedless grapes
1/4 cup honey
1/4 cup lime juice
1/4 teaspoon ginger

Combine fruits in large bowl. Mix honey, lime juice, and ginger. Pour mixture over fruit. Toss fruit salad gently and chill for several hours before serving.
    Makes six-to-eight servings.

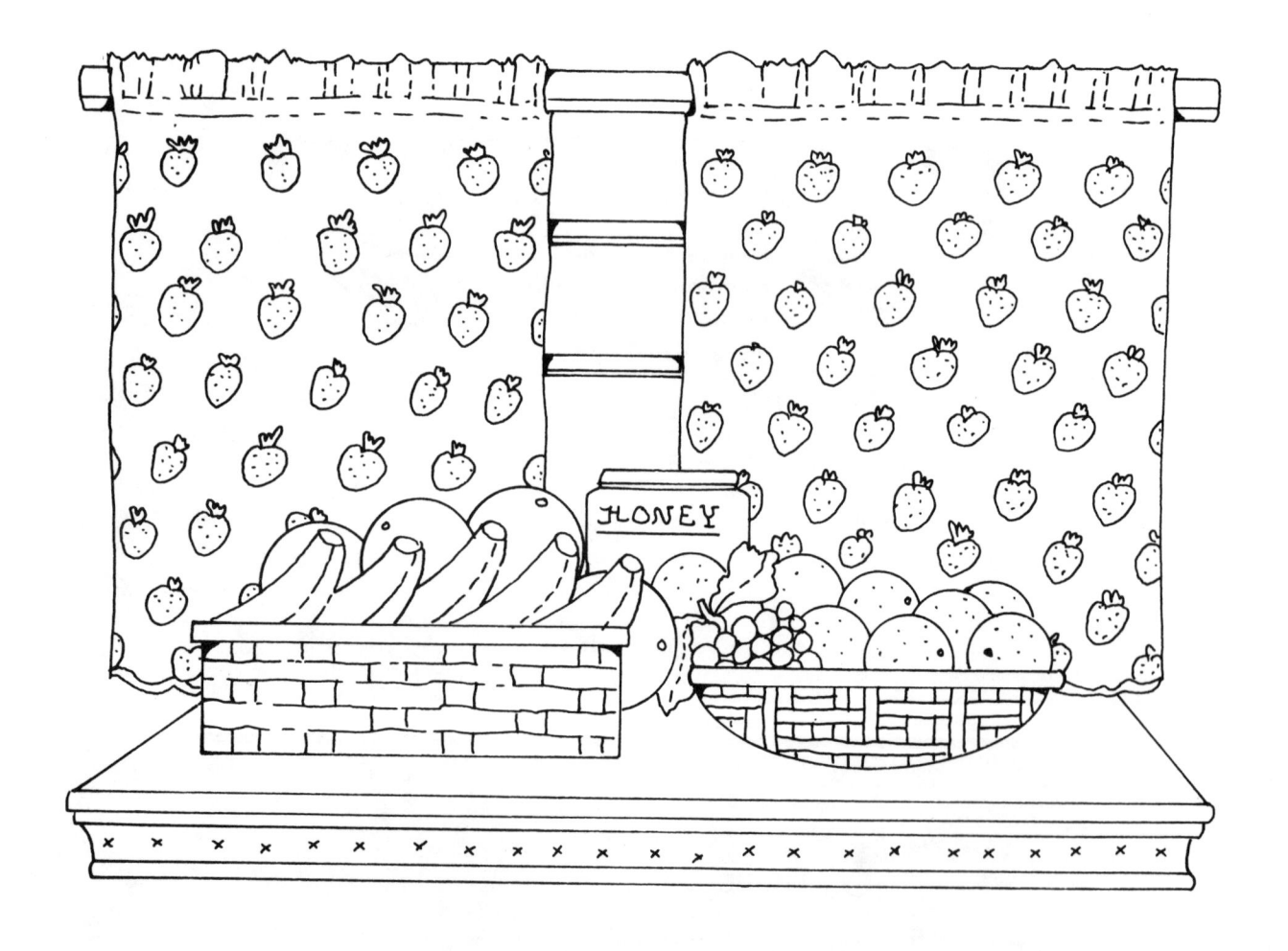

Holiday Fruit Salad

2 1/2 cups Orange-Honey Fruit Dressing
1 cup raw cranberries, chopped
2 tablespoons sugar
1 apple, cored, diced
1 grapefruit, peeled, sectioned
1/2 cup celery, diced
lettuce leaves

Put chopped cranberries in bowl and sprinkle with sugar. Combine apple, grapefruit, and celery. Add cranberries and Orange-Honey Fruit Dressing. Mix and chill. Line salad bowl with lettuce leaves and fill bowl with fruit salad.

Makes six servings.

Annie's Tips
After fruit has ripened, use as soon as possible.

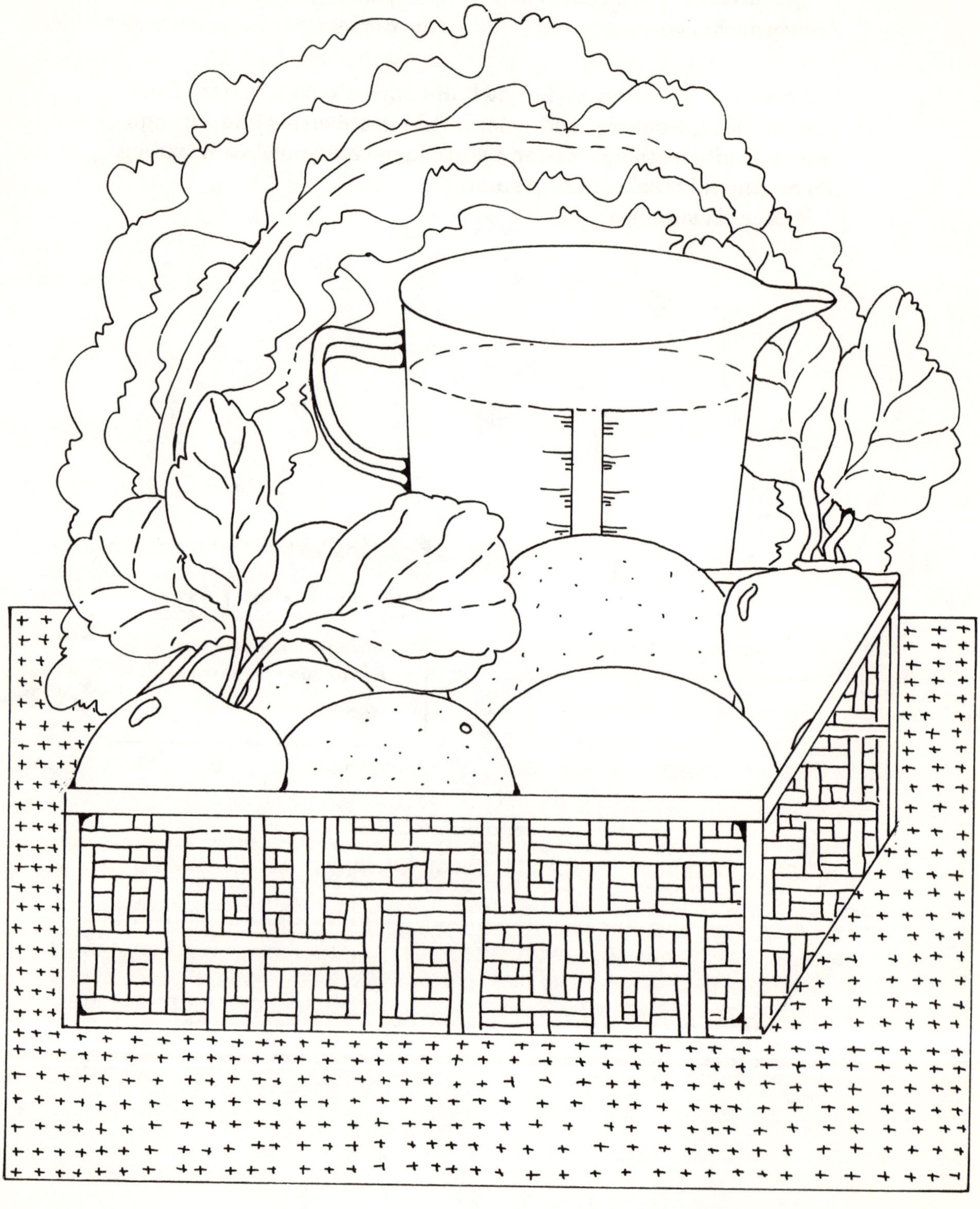

Molasses-Citrus Salad

1 1/2 cups Molasses Dressing
4 oranges, peeled, sliced crosswise
1 large Bermuda onion, sliced, separated into rings
2 beets, cooked, sliced
1 large avocado, peeled, seeded, sliced
2 grapefruits, peeled, sectioned
lettuce leaves

Line 4 chilled salad plates with lettuce. Arrange oranges, onion rings, beets, avocado, and grapefruit atop lettuce. Pour Molasses Dressing over each salad. Serve immediately.
   Makes four servings.

Pineapple Salad with Crab

1 cup Pineapple Salad Dressing
1 pound cooked lump crabmeat, picked over
1 cup cooked rice, cooled
2 apples, cored, diced
8-ounce can chunky pineapple, drained
3 tablespoons snipped dill
sprigs of dill
lettuce leaves

Combine crabmeat, rice, pineapple, apples, and snipped dill in large mixing bowl. Add 1 cup Pineapple Dressing. Toss mixture. Cover and chill for about 1 hour.
   Line deep salad bowl with lettuce leaves. Transfer crab mixture to salad bowl; garnish with sprigs of dill. Additional dressing may be served in side dish.
   Makes four servings.

Poached Naval Orange Salad

6 naval oranges, peeled, and sectioned
1 orange rind, cut very fine
2/3 cup orange juice
2/3 cup water
2/3 cup honey
lettuce leaves
1 cup yogurt

After peeling oranges remove all white membrane. Place orange rind in saucepan with water, orange juice, and honey. Simmer for 10 minutes, stirring frequently. Remove oranges from sauce and chill.

Strain sauce. Blend 2 tablespoons of sauce with yogurt. Line 6 salad plates with lettuce leaves. Arrange chilled oranges on salad plates. Spoon yogurt mixture over oranges.

Makes six servings.

Strawberry Delight

2 1/2 cups Strawberry Dressing
mint leaves
1 large honeydew, halved, seeded, fiber removed
1 pint strawberries, hulled, halved if large
1 cup seedless grapes

Peel melon and cut into wedges. Arrange melon wedges on 6 salad plates. Spoon Strawberry Dressing over melon wedges. Place strawberries and grapes on each plate atop dressing. Garnish with mint leaves.

Makes six servings.

Annie's Tips

Ripen fruit in bowl or basket at room temperature.

Stuffed Peach Salad

3/4 cup Cream Cheese Dressing
8 canned peach halves, drained
1 cup coconut
1/2 cup celery, minced

1 cup pecans, chopped
1/2 teaspoon salt
pulp from peach halves
lettuce leaves

Remove small amount of pulp from cavity of each peach. Combine pulp with coconut, celery, pecans, and salt. Chill. Arrange 2 peach halves on 4 lettuce-lined individual salad plates. Fill cavity with chilled mixture. Garnish with Cream Cheese Dressing.
    Makes four servings.

Annie's Tips
After cutting fruit, brush lightly with lemon juice to preserve color.

Stuffed Pear Salad

3/4 cup Cream Cheese Dressing
2/3 cup fresh dates, pitted, sliced
romaine leaves

8 canned pear halves, drained, sliced
1 teaspoon slivered almonds

Substitute orange juice with 1 teaspoon orange peel when preparing Cream Cheese Dressing. Add dates to dressing. Chill.
    Line 4 salad plates with romaine. Arrange two pear halves on each salad plate. Spoon cream cheese mixture into the center of each pear. Garnish with slivered almonds.
    Makes four servings.

Tossed Fruit Salad

2 cups Lemon Dressing
3 pears, peeled, cored, sliced
2 medium bananas, sliced
1 medium orange, peeled, sectioned, seeded
1 cup pineapple, chopped
1/2 cup walnuts, chopped
cinnamon
lettuce leaves

Combine fruits and walnuts in deep bowl. Toss fruits and walnuts with Lemon Dressing. Chill for several hours. Line serving bowl with lettuce leaves and fill with fruit salad. Sprinkle with cinnamon.

Makes six servings.

Yam-Fruit Salad

2 cups Pineapple Salad Dressing
5 yams, cooked, peeled, sliced
4 bananas, sliced
3 apples, cored and diced
1 cup golden raisins

Bake yams until tender but firm. Test in about 45 minutes. Peel yams while still warm. Combine diced yams, bananas, apples, and raisins. Toss salad with Pineapple Salad Dressing.
   Makes six-to-eight servings.

SALADS MADE WITH POTATOES, RICE, AND PASTA

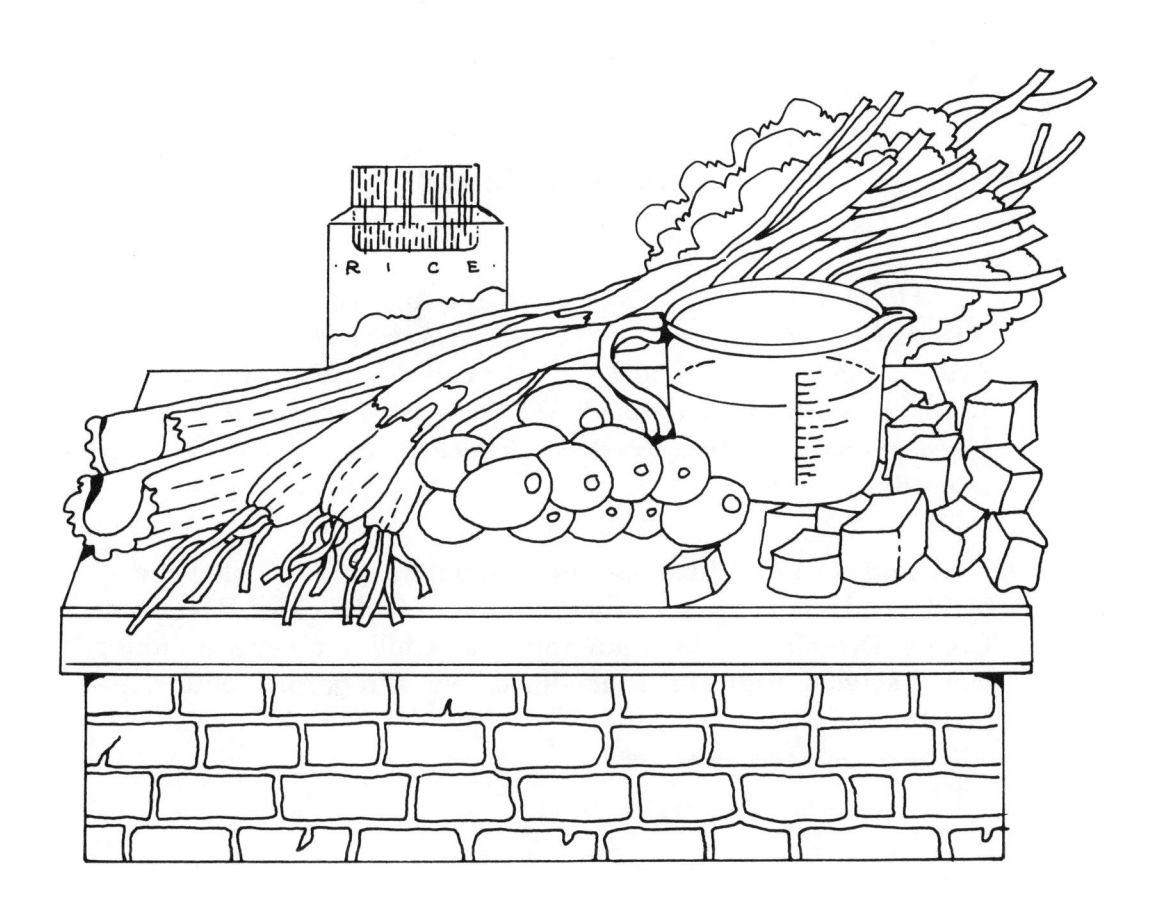

Apple Raisin Potato Salad

1 cup Quick Potato Salad Dressing
3 hard cooking apples,
  peeled and cored
2 pounds new potatoes, boiled
1/4 cup dry white wine
1/2 cup white raisins

Slice apples into 1/4-inch wedges; set aside. Cook potatoes, with skin on, in boiling salted water. Cook until tender, about 15 to 20 minutes. Drain, peel, and slice potatoes into 1/4-inch pieces while still warm. Put potatoes in deep serving dish and toss with wine.

Add apples and raisins to potatoes. Add Quick Potato Salad Dressing and toss mixture. Serve salad warm.

Makes six servings.

Bologna Salad

2 cups Pickled Beet Sour Cream
  Dressing
3 cups cooked potatoes, cubed
12 ounces chunk bologna, cubed
1 medium apple, cored and cubed
snipped parsley
1/2 cup pickled beets,
  cut in strips
1/4 cup dill pickle, chopped
1/4 cup onion, chopped
lettuce leaves

In mixing bowl, combine potatoes, bologna, apple, pickled beets, pickle, and onion. Toss gently to combine. Add Pickled Beet Sour Cream Dressing to bologna mixture. Chill for several hours before serving. Serve in lettuce-lined bowl and garnish with snipped parsley.

Makes about six servings.

Chicken and Brown Rice Toss

3/4 cup Herbed Sour Cream Dressing
3 cups cooked brown rice
2 cups cooked chicken, cubed
1/2 cup celery, sliced
1/4 cup pitted ripe olives, sliced
2 tablespoons green onion, diced
1/2 cup cashew nuts, chopped coarsely
lettuce leaves

Combine cooked rice, chicken, celery, olives, and onion in large mixing bowl. Add Herbed Sour Cream Dressing. Toss mixture gently to coat. Cover bowl and chill for several hours. Before serving, add cashews and toss again. Turn mixture into lettuce-lined salad bowl.

Makes four-to-five servings.

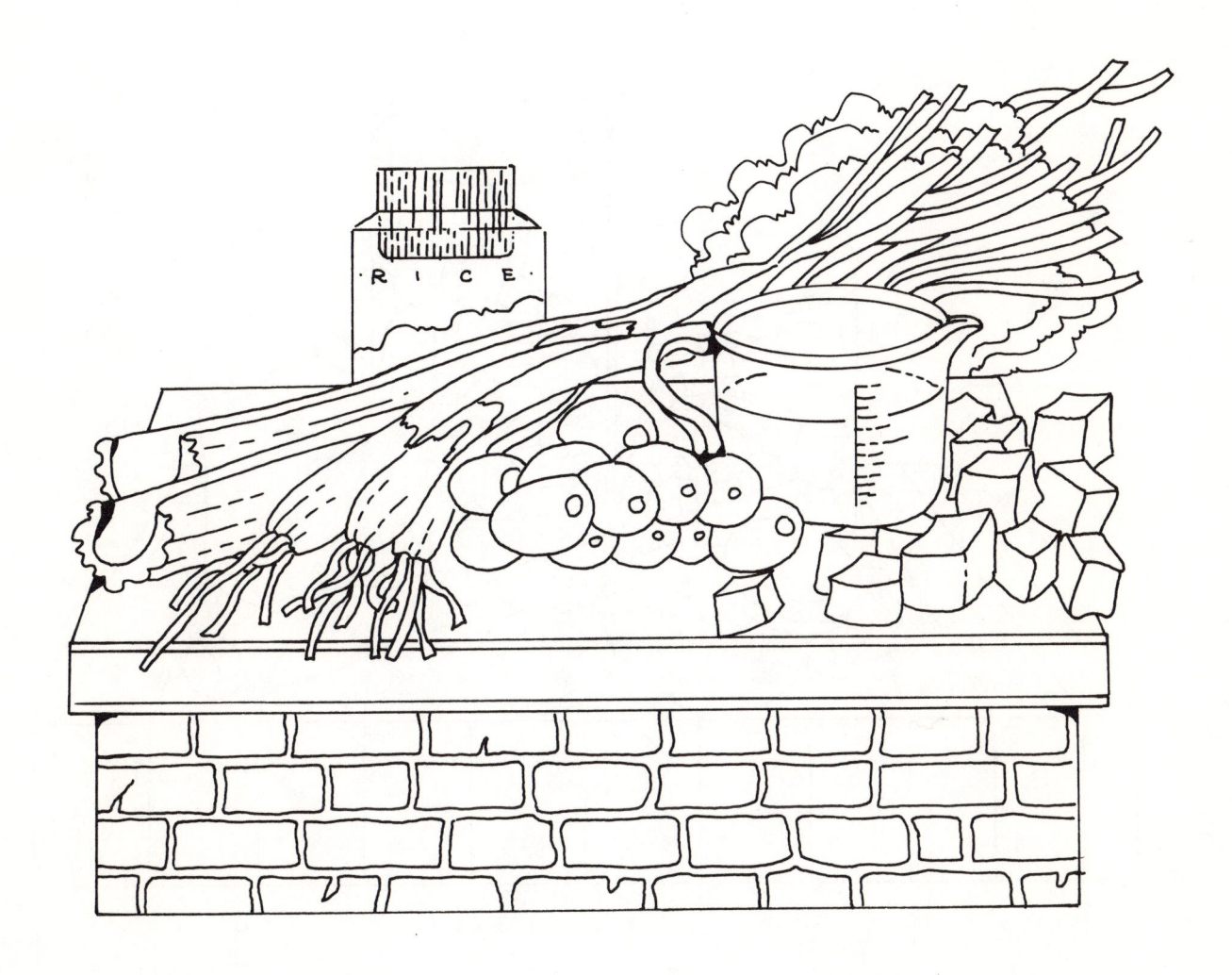

Chicken-Potato Salad

1 1/2 cups Creamy Salad
　Dressing
4 cups cooked potatoes, cubed
1/2 cup cooked chicken, cubed
8 ounces Swiss cheese,
　cut in strips

1/2 cup diced celery
1/2 cup green onion, sliced
1/2 cup radish, sliced
1/4 cup green pepper, chopped
3 hard-boiled eggs, diced
1/2 teaspoon salt

Gently toss all ingredients in large bowl; cover. Chill for several hours.
　Makes six servings.

Annie's Tips
Cook potatoes until just tender. Never overcook.

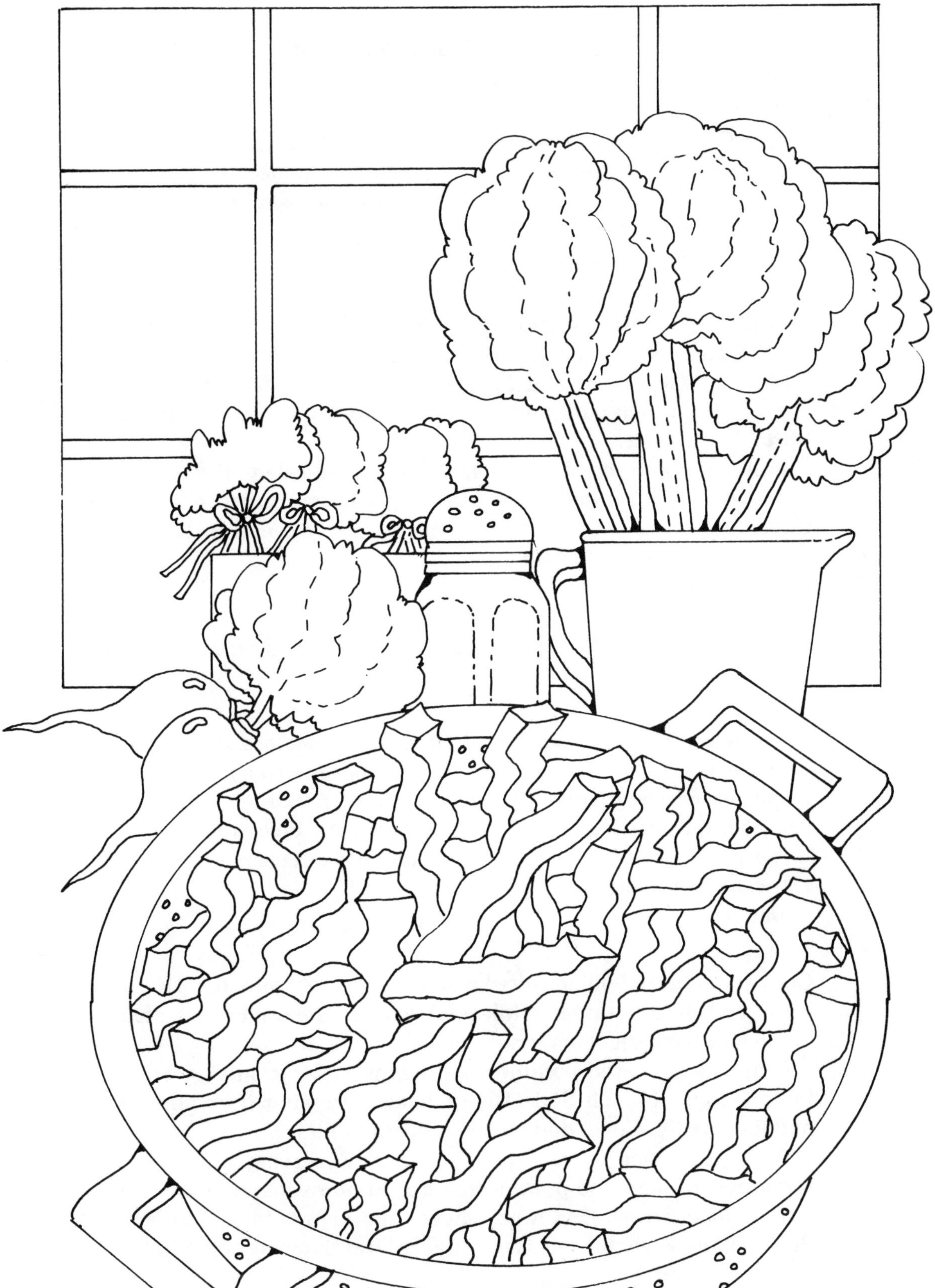

French Fry Potato Salad

3/4 cup Creamy Bacon Dressing
one 16-ounce package frozen
　French fried potatoes
1 1/2 teaspoons salt
4 hard-boiled eggs, chopped

1/2 cup radishes, sliced
1/2 cup celery, diced
2 tablespoons parsley
lettuce leaves

In a large pot, bring 4 cups of water to full boil. Carefully drop frozen fries into boiling water. Remove pot from heat immediately. Cover pot and let stand for 4 to 5 minutes. Drain potatoes into collander and spread potatoes onto paper towels. Sprinkle with salt.

In a large bowl, combine eggs, radishes, and celery. Add cooled potatoes. Add Creamy Bacon Dressing and toss mixture gently. Cover bowl and chill for several hours. Serve salad in lettuce-lined bowl and garnish with parsley.

Makes eight servings.

French-Style Bean and Potato Salad

1 cup French-Style Blue Cheese
　Dressing
1 small head iceberg lettuce
6 medium red potatoes,
　cooked, peeled
1/2 pound French-style
　green beans

4 medium tomatoes, quartered
one 7-ounce can tuna,
　drained, flaked
12 pitted black olives
2 tablespoons capers

Cook potatoes in boiling salted water for 15 to 20 minutes. Drain, peel, and dice potatoes while still warm. Steam French-style green beans until just tender.

Combine prepared potatoes and beans in large mixing bowl. Pour 1/2 cup French-Style Blue Cheese Dressing over mixture and toss gently. Cover and chill for several hours.

Arrange lettuce leaves on large shallow serving plate. Add tomatoes to bean and potato mixture. Spoon vegetable mixture onto lettuce leaves. Add tuna, olives, and capers to salad plate. Pour 1/2 cup French-Style Blue Cheese Dressing over top of salad and serve at once.

Makes four-to-six servings.

Annie's Tips
Pasta should be cooked al dente (8-to-10 minutes).

Garden Macaroni Salad

1 cup Herbed Sour Cream Dressing
4 cups cooked elbow macaroni, drained
1 cup cucumber, seeded and diced
1 cup celery, sliced
1/4 cup green pepper, diced
1/4 cup radishes, sliced thin
2 tablespoons scallions, sliced
2 tomatoes, seeded and diced
lettuce leaves

Gently toss together all ingerdients. Cover and chill for several hours before serving. Serve in lettuce-lined salad bowl.
   Makes about six servings.

Annie's Tips

To refresh, plunge hot food into cold water to quickly stop the cooking process and avoid over-cooking.

Hot Potato Salad

3 pounds red potatoes, boiled
3/4 cup onion, minced
1/4 cup celery, minced
1/2 cup white wine vinegar
1 tablespoon sugar
salt
pepper
6 strips, bacon, crumbled
3/4 teaspoon celery seed
1/4 cup parsley, minced

Cook potato, with skin on, in boiling salted water in covered pot. Cook until tender, about 25 minutes. Drain, peel, and slice potatoes while still warm and set aside.

Sauté onion and celery in small amount of cooking oil for 1 minute. Add broth and vinegar. Season with sugar, salt, and pepper to taste. Add onion and celery mixture to potatoes. Add crumbled bacon, celery seed, and parsley. Toss and serve immediately.

Makes eight servings.

Macaroni and Cheese Salad

1 cup Special Yogurt Dressing
4 cups cooked elbow macaroni, drained
2 cups leftover ham, cut into cubes
1/2 cup aged Swiss cheese, cubed
1/2 cup mung bean sprouts
lettuce leaves

Gently toss all ingredients together. Cover and chill for several hours before serving. Serve in lettuce-lined salad bowl.

Makes about six servings.

Annie's Tips
Pasta should be cooked al dente (8-to-10 minutes).

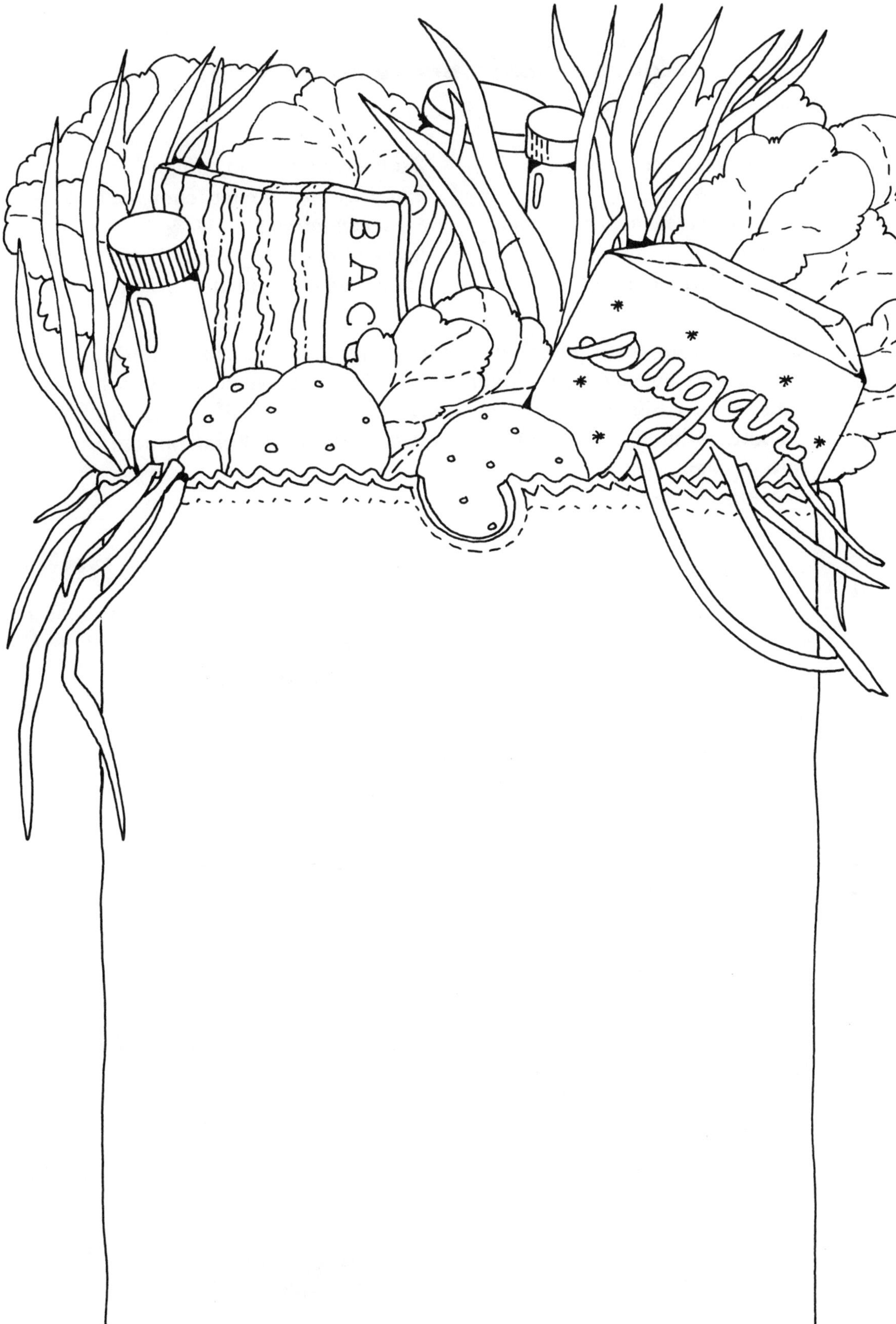
BAC
Sugar

Macaroni and Cheese Salad Ring

2 1/4 cups Ginger Cheese Dressing
4 cups cooked elbow macaroni, drained
1/4 cup pimento, diced
2 tablespoons onion, chopped
2 tablespoons parsley, chopped
3/4 teaspoon salt
lettuce leaves
additional pimento and parsley

Combine macaroni and dressing in large bowl. Stir in pimento, onion, parsley, and salt. Cover bowl or press mixture into 9-inch ring mold. Chill several hours. Loosen sides with knife. Turn out on lettuce-lined serving plate. Garnish with additional pimento and parsley.
    Makes six servings.

Annie's Tips
Pasta should be cooked al dente (8-to-10 minutes).

Macaroni Slaw

1 cup Yogurt Slaw Dressing
4 cups cooked elbow macaroni, drained
3 cups green cabbage, finely shredded
1 cup carrot, coarsely shredded
1/2 cup green pepper, finely chopped
3 tablespoons onion, minced

Gently toss all ingredients except dressing. Add Yogurt Slaw Dressing to tossed ingredients. Stir gently until coated. Cover container and chill for several hours.
    Makes seven servings.

Annie's Tips
Cook pasta and potatoes in salted boiling water.

Pepper Steak Salad

1 cup Caper Dressing
1 cup cooked long-grain or
 brown rice
2 cups cooked beef,
 sliced thin and cut in strips
3 cups torn mixed salad greens

one 15 1/4-ounce can pineapple
 chunks, packed in natural juice
3 medium tomatoes, cut in wedges
1 green pepper, cut in strips
1/2 cup mung bean sprouts

Place beef in bowl. Pour Caper Dressing over beef. Cover and marinate for several hours in refrigerator. Place cooked rice in small mixing bowl; set aside.

To serve, place salad greens in large salad bowl. Drain marinade from beef into small mixing bowl with rice. Stir rice mixture. Put rice atop salad greens in a mound. Top with beef, pineapple chunks, tomato, green pepper, and sprouts. Salad is ready to be served or may be tossed lightly.

Makes four servings.

Sweetcorn Salad

1/2 cup White Wine Dressing
2-3 drops Tabasco® sauce
1/2 teaspoon dry mustard
1 bay leaf
1 pound canned sweetcorn, drained

1 small green pepper, seeded, finely chopped
4 canned pimientos, drained, finely chopped
1 small onion, finely chopped

Combine Tabasco® sauce, dry mustard, bay leaf, and White Wine Dressing in mixing bowl. Combine sweetcorn, green pepper, pimientos, and onion in salad bowl.

Pour dressing mixture over sweetcorn mixture. Cover salad bowl and set aside at room temperature for at least 2 hours. Remove and discard bay leaf before serving.

Makes four-to-six servings.

Tuna-Fruit Sea Shell Salad

1 cup Yogurt Dressing Supreme
4 cups cooked sea-shell
   macaroni, drained
one 7-ounce can tuna,
   drained and flaked
lettuce leaves

1 medium orange,
   peeled, seeded, and sectioned
1 medium apple,
   cored and sliced thin
1/3 cup dark seedless raisins

Gently toss together all ingredients. Cover and chill for several hours before serving. Serve in lettuce-lined salad bowl.
   Makes about six servings.

Annie's Tips

After cooking pasta, pour 1 cup cold water into pot; drain in collander and rinse quickly to wash off excess starch.

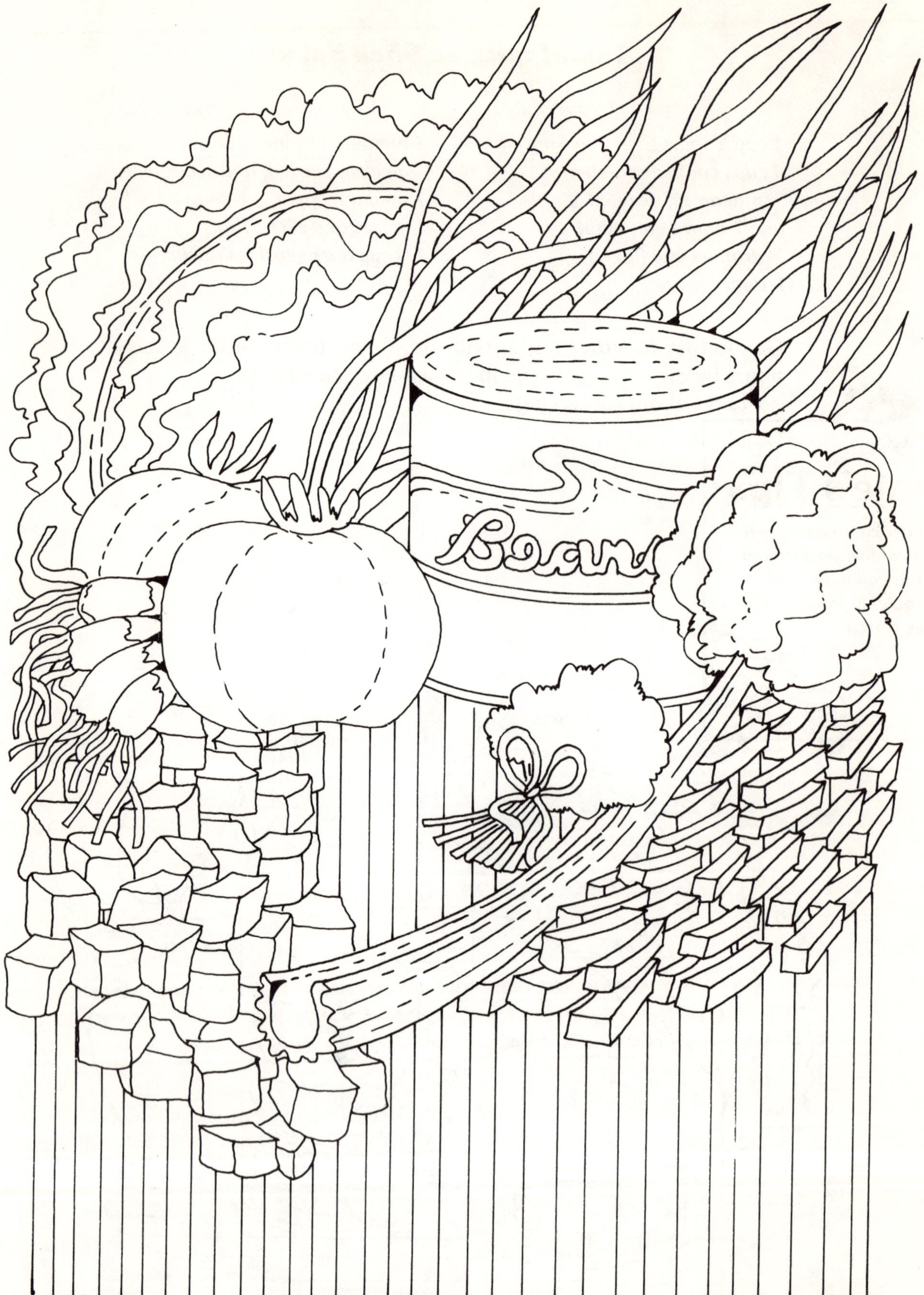
Beans

Turkey and Garbanzo Bean Toss

1 cup Peppered Avocado Dressing
one 15-ounce can garbanzo beans
2 cups cooked turkey, diced
1 cup celery, sliced
1/2 cup green pepper, chopped
1/4 cup green onion, chopped

1 medium tomato,
   seeded and diced
lettuce leaves
2 ounces Monterey Jack cheese,
   cut in strips
2 tablespoons snipped parsley

Rinse beans in cold water; drain. In large mixing bowl, combine beans, turkey, celery, green pepper, onion, and tomato. Fold Peppered Avocado Dressing into bean mixture. Cover bowl and chill for several hours.

   To serve, pour mixture into lettuce-lined salad bowl. Top with cheese and parsley.

   Makes four servings.

Vegetable Rice Salad

1 cup Special Yogurt Dressing
one 6-ounce package long-grain
   and wild rice
1 cup celery, diced
1 cup tomato, cubed

1/2 cup cucumber, diced
2 tablespoons parsley, chopped
1/2 cup soy nuts, chopped
lettuce leaves

Cook rice as directed on package; omit butter or margarine.

   Toss all ingredients together, except soy nuts. Cover bowl and chill for several hours. Line salad bowl with lettuce. Fill bowl with rice mixture. Garnish with soy nuts.

   Makes six servings.

SALADS MADE IN MOLDS

Avocado-Tuna Salad Ring

3 envelopes unflavored gelatin
1/4 cup lemon juice
3 avocados, peeled, seeded, and mashed
1 cup sour cream
1 cup mayonnaise
1/2 small onion, grated
1 tablespoon Worcestershire sauce
1 teaspoon celery salt
1/8 teaspoon pepper
lettuce leaves
tuna salad
5-cup ring mold

Dissolve unflavored gelatin in 1 cup boiling water. In mixing bowl, combine lemon juice, avocado, sour cream, mayonnaise, onion, Worcestershire, celery salt, and pepper. Blend mixture with electric mixer. Add gelatin to avocado mixture. Blend again. Pour gelatin and avocado mixture into mold. Chill until firm, about 3 to 4 hours.

Unmold onto lettuce-lined serving plate. Fill center of mold with tuna salad.

Makes eight servings.

Annie's Tips
Use paper towel and small amount of mayonnaise to coat mold.

Annie's Tips
For best results always use size and shape of mold suggested in recipe.

Beet Cucumber Salad Ring

1 cup Cool Cucumber Sauce
one 16-ounce can shoestring beets
1 envelope unflavored gelatin
1/4 cup sugar
dash salt
3 tablespoons lemon juice
1/2 small cucumber, sliced thin
lettuce leaves
3 1/2- or 4-cup ring mold

Drain beets, reserving liquid; set aside. Combine gelatin, sugar, and salt in small saucepan. Add enough water to beet liquid to make 1 3/4 cups. Add liquid to gelatin mixture. Cook and stir over low heat until gelatin dissolves. Stir in lemon juice.

Pour about 3/4 cup of gelatin mixture into ring mold. Arrange cucumbers in bottom of mold. Chill both gelatin mixtures until larger amount is partially set. Stir beets into larger amount of gelatin. Spoon over cucumbers in mold. Chill until firm. Unmold onto lettuce-lined serving plates. Serve with Cool Cucumber Sauce.

Makes six servings.

Cider Salad Mold

Fresh Fruit Dressing
4 cups apple cider
4 whole cloves
4 inches stick cinnamon
two 3-ounce packages lemon-flavored gelatin
1 orange, peeled, seeded, sectioned
1 unpared apple, cored, diced
lettuce leaves
5 1/2-cup ring mold

In saucepan, combine cider, cloves, and cinnamon. Cover saucepan and simmer for 15 minutes; strain. Dissolve gelatin in hot cider. Pour 1 cup of cider mixture into mold. Chill until partially set. Keep remaining gelatin at room temperature.

Arrange orange sections over gelatin in mold. Chill again until almost firm. Also chill remaining gelatin until partially set. Fold apples into partially-set gelatin. Carefully spoon mixture into mold. Chill until firm.

Unmold onto lettuce-lined plate. Fill center of cider salad mold with Fresh Fruit Dressing.

Makes eight servings.

Cottage Cheese Peach Salad

one 3-ounce package peach-flavored gelatin
1/2 cup canned peach slices, drained and diced
lettuce leaves
1 cup creamed cottage cheese
4 tablespoons sour cream
slivered almonds
    or chopped chives
4 individual-sized molds

Dissolve gelatin in 1 cup boiling water. Add 3/4 cup cold water or reserved juice from peaches. Chill until partially set. Fold peaches into gelatin. Spoon gelatin mixture into molds. Chill until firm.

Line 4 individual dessert dishes with lettuce. Place 1/4 cup cottage cheese into each dish. Unmold gelatins atop cottage cheese. Garnish each mold with 1 tablespoon sour cream. Top with almonds or chives.

Makes four servings.

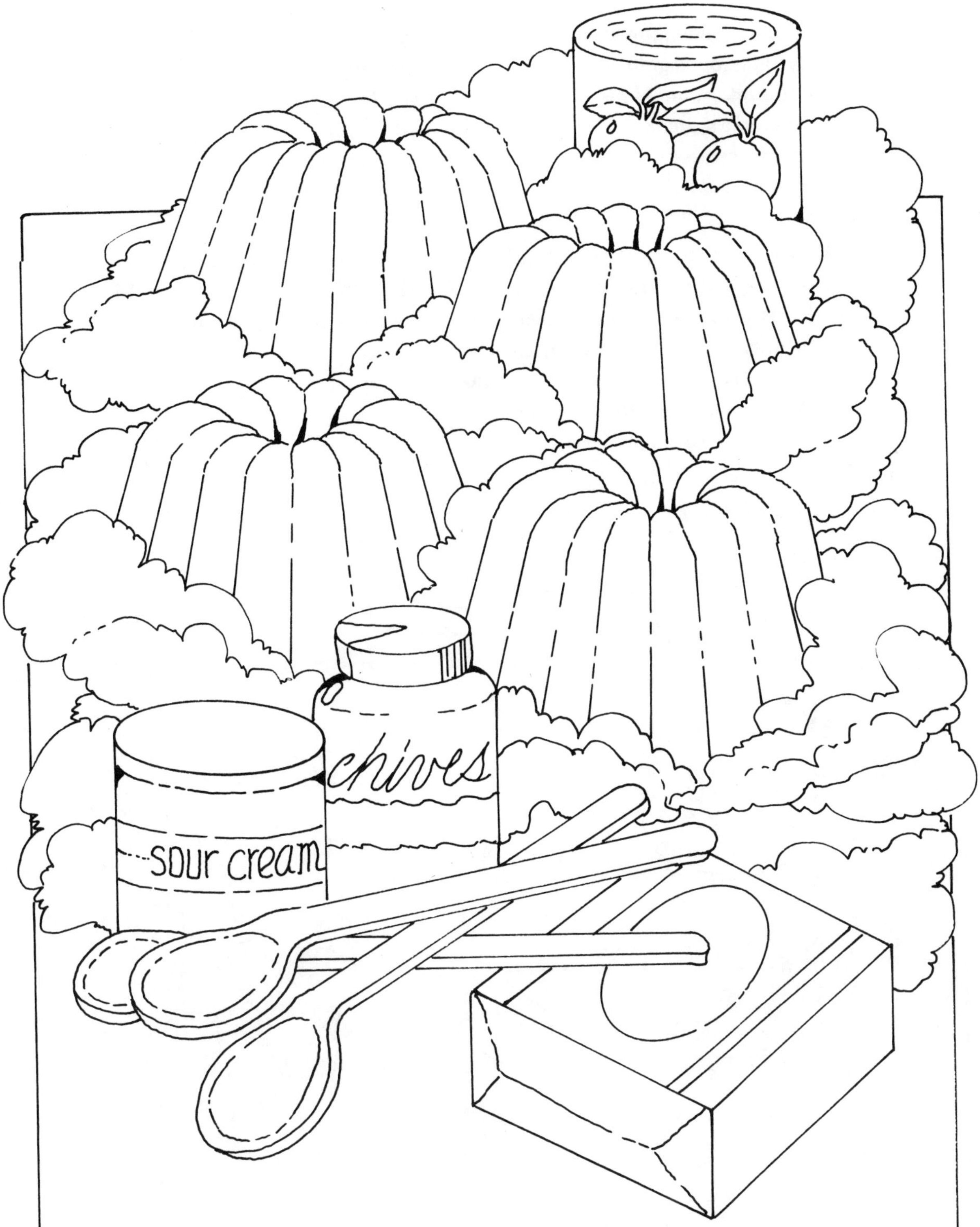
chives
sour cream

Cran-Apple Turkey Salad Mold

one 6-ounce package straw-
 berry-flavored gelatin
one 16-ounce can whole
 cranberry sauce
1 cup applesauce
1/2 cup port wine

1/4 cup walnuts, chopped
1/4 cup apple, peeled, chopped
lettuce leaves
sliced turkey
6 1/2-cup mold

Dissolve gelatin in 2 cups boiling water. Stir cranberry sauce, applesauce, and wine into gelatin. Chill until partially set. Fold walnuts and apples into gelatin. Pour mixture into mold and chill until firm, about 6 hours or overnight. Unmold onto lettuce-lined platter. Arrange turkey around mold.
 Makes ten-to-twelve servings.

Cucumber and Grape Salad

two 3-ounce packages lemon-
 flavored gelatin
3 tablespoons orange juice
6 tablespoons lemon juice
1 tablespoon onion,
 very finely chopped
1/8 teaspoon cayenne pepper
1/2 teaspoon salt
1 large cucumber,
 peeled, thinly sliced
1 pound seedless white grapes,
 halved
lettuce leaves
6-cup mold

Dissolve gelatin in 2 1/2 cups boiling water. Stir in orange juice and lemon juice. Add onion, cayenne, and salt. Chill until mixture is partially set.

Reserve 10 cucumber slices and 10 grapes. Set aside. Fold remaining cucumber and grapes into gelatin mixture. Spoon mixture into mold. Chill until firm.

Arrange lettuce leaves on serving plate. Unmold gelatin onto lettuce leaves. Garnish salad with reserved cucumber slices and grapes.

Makes eight servings.

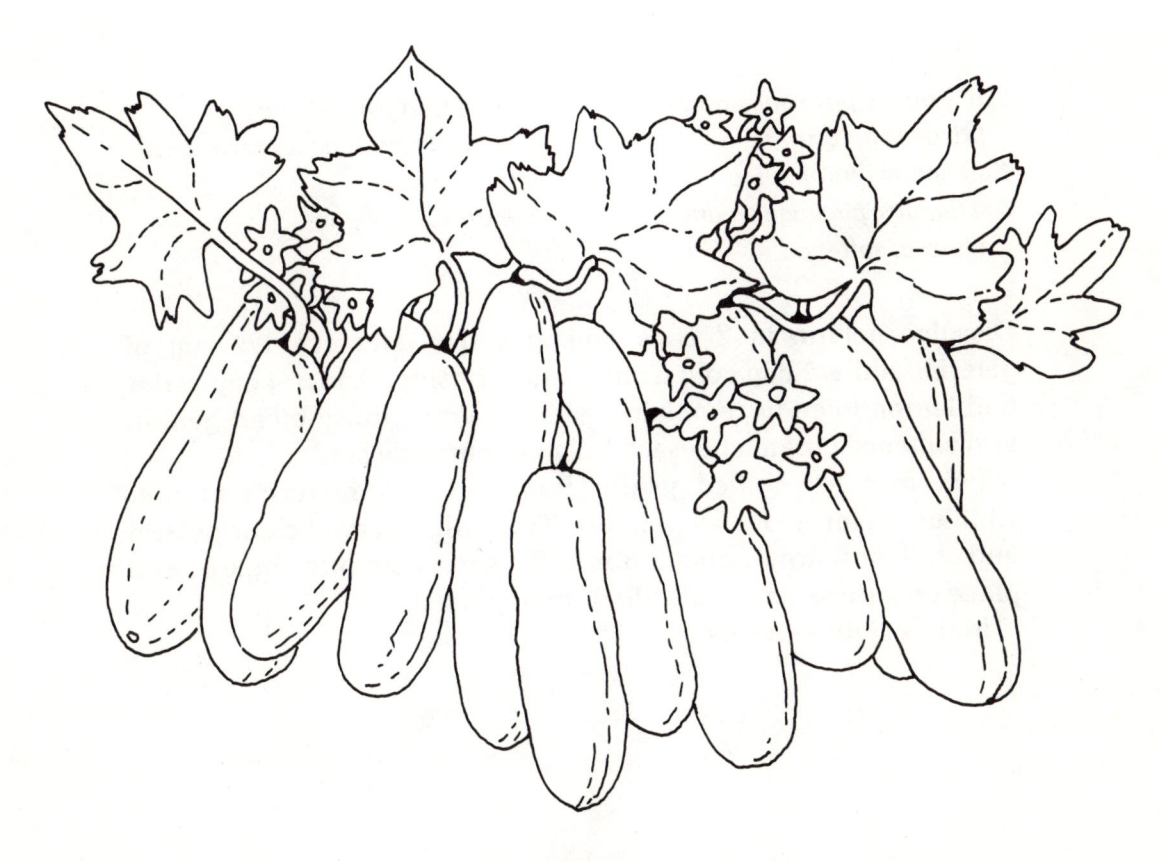

Frozen Fruitcake Salad

1 cup sour cream
4 tablespoons cherry yogurt
2 tablespoons lemon juice
1/2 cup sugar
1 teaspoon vanilla
one 13-ounce can crushed
  pineapple, drained
lettuce leaves

2 medium bananas, diced
1/2 cup red candied cherries,
  halved
1/2 cup green candied cherries,
  halved
1/2 cup walnuts, chopped
4 1/2-cup ring mold

In mixing bowl, blend together sour cream, yogurt, sugar, lemon juice, and vanilla. Fold in fruit and nuts. Pour into ring mold. Freeze for several hours or overnight. Unmold onto lettuce-lined plate. Let stand for 10 minutes before serving.
   Makes eight servings.

Fruit Squares

two 3-ounce packages lime-
  flavored gelatin
1 teaspoon lemon juice
one 8-ounce package cream
  cheese, softened

1 cup fresh fruit, diced
  (strawberries, peaches, grapes)
lettuce leaves
8-inch square pan

Dissolve gelatin in 2 cups boiling water. Reserve 1/2 cup of gelatin, add 1/2 cup cold water, and set aside. Add 3/4 cup water and lemon juice to remaining gelatin. Very slowly blend gelatin into softened cream cheese. Chill until partially set.
   Fold fruit into chilled gelatin. Spoon gelatin mixture into pan. Chill again for about 15 minutes. Top with reserved clear gelatin and chill until firm, about 3 hours. To serve, cut into squares and place on lettuce-lined individual salad plates.
   Makes eight servings.

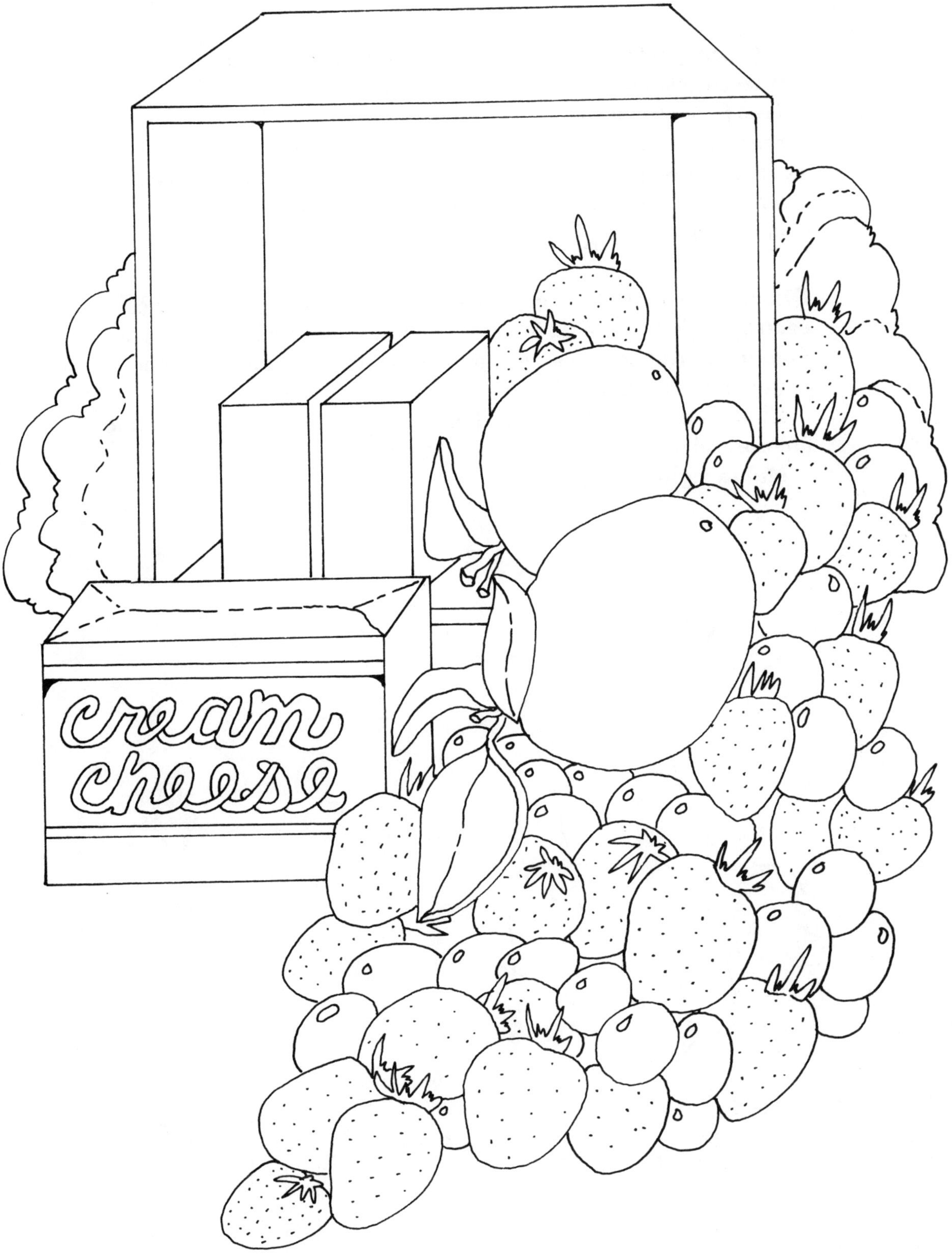
cream
cheese

Grapefruit Ring

two 3-ounce packages lemon-
    flavored gelatin
1/3 cup frozen lemonade
    concentrate
1 cup red grapes,
    halved and seeded
chopped celery tops

2 grapefruits, peeled, seeded,
    and sectioned
1/2 cup celery, chopped
creamed cottage cheese,
    enough to fill center of mold
6-cup ring mold

Dissolve gelatin in 1 1/2 cups boiling water. Stir in lemonade concentrate and 2 cups cold water. Chill until mixture is partially set. Fold grapefruit sections, grapes, and celery into mixture. Spoon gelatin mixture into mold.

Chill until firm. Unmold. Fill center of mold with cottage cheese and garnish with chopped celery tops.

Makes eight servings.

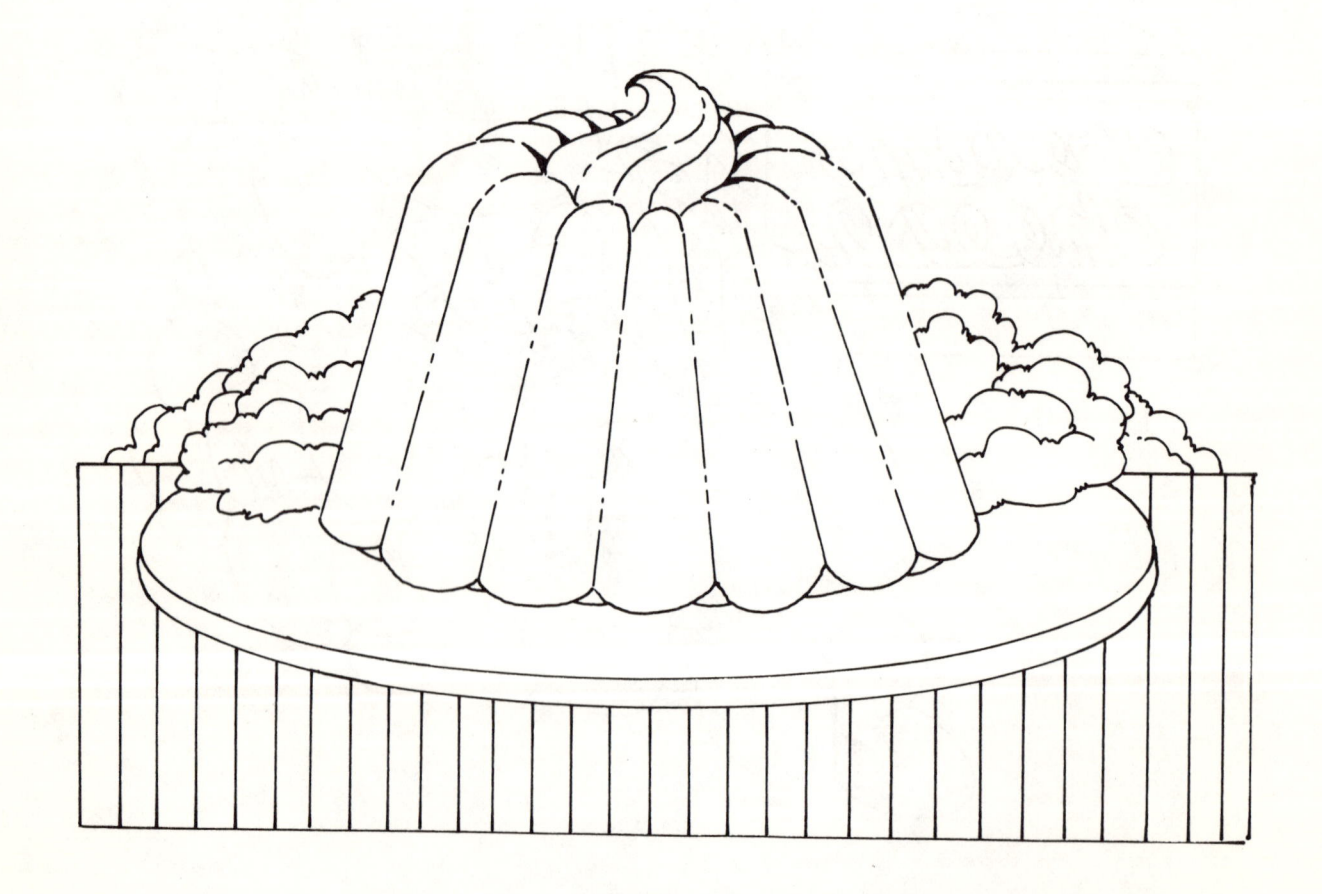

Lime-Walnut Salad

one 3-ounce package lime-flavored gelatin
1 cup crushed pineapple with syrup
2 stalks celery, chopped
one 12-ounce carton creamed cottage cheese
1/2 cup walnuts, chopped fine
5-cup mold

Dissolve gelatin in 1 cup boiling water. Add pineapple with syrup to gelatin. Chill until partially set. Beat cottage cheese with electric mixer for 1 minute. Add gelatin to cottage cheese. Mix until well blended. Add celery and walnuts to gelatin mixture. Pour into mold. Chill until firm.

Makes six servings.

Annie's Tips
Substitute water with fruit juice whenever reserved juice is available.

Molded Vegetable Salad

two 3-ounce packages lemon-
   flavored gelatin
2 teaspoons salt
3 tablespoons lemon juice
1/2 cup cucumber,
   seeded and diced
1/2 cup cooked peas
1/2 cup cooked carrots
2 tablespoons pimento, chopped
lettuce leaves
5-cup mold

Dissolve gelatin and salt in 2 cups boiling water. Pour lemon juice into measuring cup. Add enough water to equal 1 1/2 cups. Add to gelatin. Chill mixture until partially set. Fold cucumber, peas, carrots, and pimento into gelatin. Pour mixture into mold. Chill until firm, about 4 hours. Unmold onto lettuce-lined serving plate.
   Makes eight servings.

Molded Waldorf Salad

1 2/3 cups Zesty Blue Cheese
   Dressing
one 3-ounce package lime-
   flavored-gelatin
1/2 cup sauterne
2 tablespoons lemon juice
1/2 cup celery, chopped
1/4 cup walnuts
1 red apple, cored, diced
lettuce leaves
3-cup mold

Dissolve lime-flavored gelatin in 1 1/4 cups boiling water. Add sauterne and lemon juice. Chill until partially set. Add celery, walnuts, and apple. Pour into mold and chill until firm. Unmold onto lettuce leaves, and serve with a side dish of Zesty Blue Cheese Dressing.
   Makes four-to-six servings.

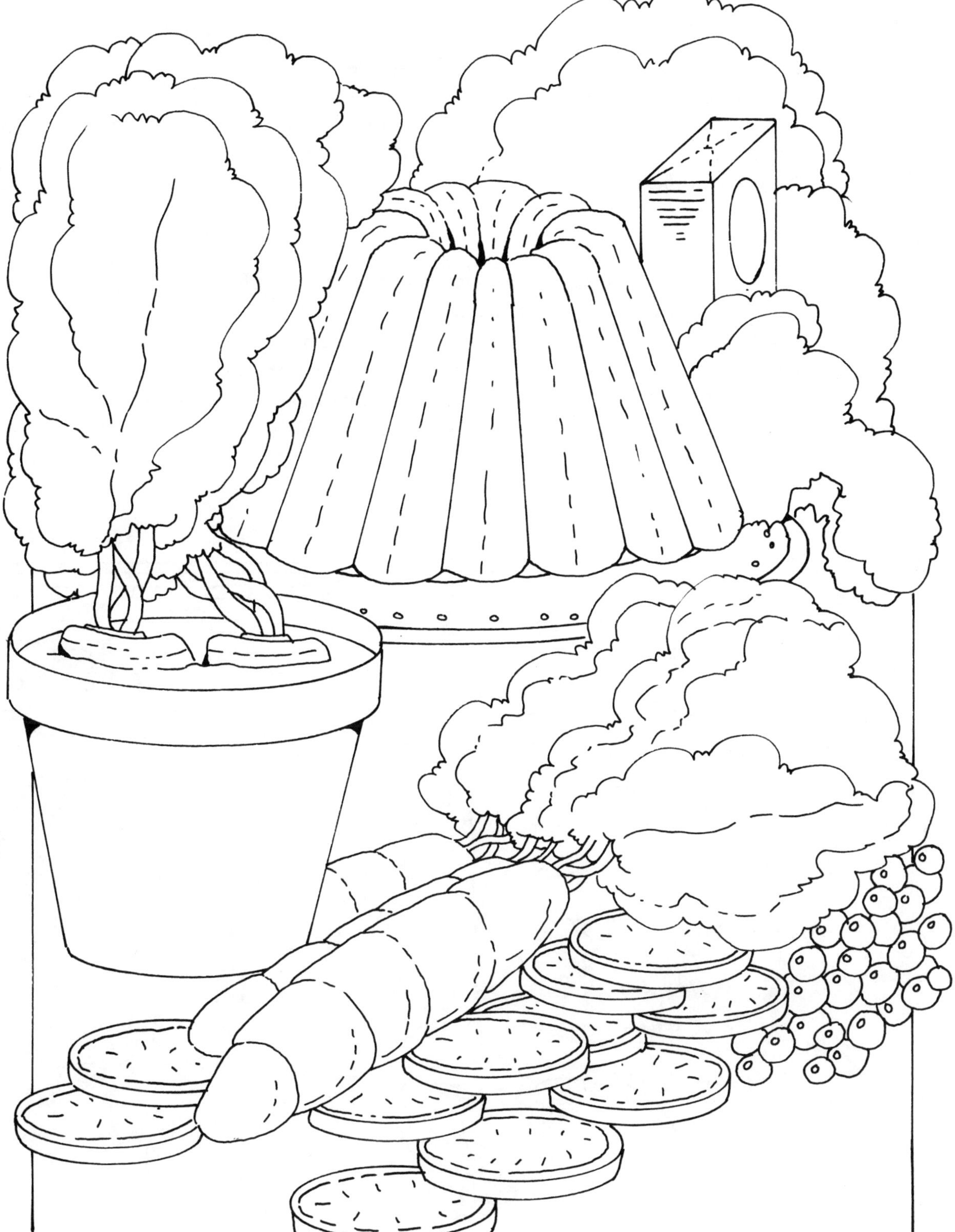

Pear Cucumber Mold

one 3-ounce package lime-
 flavored-gelatin
2 tablespoons lemon juice
2 cups canned pears, drained,
 chopped
3/4 cup cucumbers,
 chopped fine
1 cup cream-style cottage
 cheese
lettuce leaves
1 cucumber, sliced thin
2 tablespoons minced chives
4-cup ring mold

Dissolve gelatin in 1 cup boiling water. Add lemon juice and 1 cup cold water. Chill until partially set.

Add pears and cucumbers to gelatin. Pour mixture into mold and chill until firm, about 3 hours. Unmold onto lettuce-lined salad plate. Fill center of mold with cottage cheese. Garnish cottage cheese with chives. Arrange sliced cucumbers around mold.

Makes four-to-six servings.

Pear and Lime Salad Mold

one 16-ounce can Bartlett pears, drained and diced
1 package lime-flavored gelatin
2/3 cup reserved pear juice
1/4 cup lemon juice
1/4 teaspoon salt
1/4 cup pimento, diced
1 cup cabbage, finely shredded
lettuce leaves
6 individual-sized molds

Drain canned pears and reserve the juice. Dissolve gelatin in 1 cup boiling water. Add reserved pear juice, lemon juice, and salt to gelatin. Chill until partially set.

Add pears, pimento, and cabbage to gelatin. Pour into individual molds and chill until set. Unmold onto lettuce-lined salad plates.

Makes six servings.

Annie's Tips
Partially set means the consistency of unbeaten egg whites.

Red Top Egg Salad

one 3-ounce package lemon-flavored gelatin
1/4 cup lemon juice
1/2 cup mayonnaise
1/2 teaspoon salt
one 13 1/2-ounce can tomato aspic
6 hard-boiled eggs, chopped
1/2 cup celery, minced
1/2 cup carrot, grated
2 tablespoons snipped parsley
1/2 teaspoon onion, finely grated
lettuce leaves
1 hard-boiled egg, sliced
6-cup mold

Dissolve gelatin in 1 cup boiling water. Add 1/2 cup cold water and lemon juice to gelatin. Chill until partially set.

Melt aspic in saucepan over low heat. Add 1/4 cup water. Pour aspic into mold. Set mold aside; do not chill.

Fold chopped eggs, carrot, parsley, and onion into partially-set lemon gelatin. Carefully spoon gelatin and egg mixture atop the aspic; chill until firm, about 4 to 6 hours. Unmold onto lettuce-lined salad plate and garnish with sliced egg.

Makes six servings.

Sangria Salad

2 envelopes unflavored gelatin
1/2 cup sugar
1 1/2 cups water
1 1/4 cups rosé wine
1 cup orange juice
2 tablespoons lemon juice

3 oranges, peeled, seeded, sectioned
1 large apple, cored, cut into chunks
1 cup red grapes, halved and seeded
6 1/2-cup mold

In saucepan, combine gelatin and sugar. Stir in 1 1/2 cups water. Cook and stir until gelatin dissolves. Remove saucepan from heat. Stir rosé wine, orange juice, and lemon juice into gelatin mixture. Chill until partially set.

Pour about 2 cups gelatin into mold and top with orange sections. Alternate remaining gelatin with apples and grapes. Chill until firm. Unmold. Garnish with additional grapes, if desired.

Makes eight-to-ten servings.

Seafood Salad

1 envelope unflavored gelatin
3 tablespoons lemon juice
1/4 teaspoon salt
dash cayenne
3/4 cup mayonnaise
2 hard-boiled eggs, chopped
1 cup celery, chopped

1/2 cup tiny cooked shrimp
one 7-ounce can crabmeat, all cartilage removed
lettuce leaves
1 cup small cooked shrimp, peeled and cleaned
5-cup ring mold

Dissolve gelatin in 2/3 cup boiling water. Add lemon juice, salt, cayenne, and mayonnaise to gelatin. Chill until partially set. In bowl, combine eggs, celery, tiny shrimp, and crabmeat. Add gelatin mixture.

Pour into mold and chill until firm. Unmold onto lettuce leaves. Fill center of mold with cooked shrimp.

Makes six-to-eight servings.

Annie's Tip

Almost firm means gelatin feels sticky to the touch.

Spiced Peach Salad

one 29-ounce can peaches
4 medium oranges
2 teaspoons allspice
one 6-ounce package lemon-
    flavored gelatin

1/2 cup pecans, chopped
1/2 cup maraschino cherries
lettuce leaves
8-cup mold

Drain peaches and reserve syrup. Chop peaches. Peel and section the oranges over a bowl to catch the juice. Combine the juice with reserved syrup. If necessary add enough water to measure 2 cups. Set aside.

Dissolve gelatin in 2 cups boiling water. Add allspice to gelatin. Add the 2 cups of juice and syrup combination. Chill until partially set.

Add peaches, orange sections, pecans, and cherries to gelatin. Pour into mold and chill for about 6 hours or overnight. Unmold onto lettuce-lined serving plate.

Makes ten-to-twelve servings.

Strawberry Yogurt Mold

2 envelopes unflavored gelatin
1 cup lemonade
2 cups ginger ale
3/4 cup strawberry yogurt
1/4 teaspoon salt
6-cup mold

1 1/2 cups fresh strawberries, hulled and sliced
1/4 cup slivered blanched almonds
1 cup fresh whole strawberries, hulled

Heat lemonade in saucepan. Stir in gelatin until dissolved. Pour gelatin into large bowl. Add ginger ale, yogurt, and salt. Beat gelatin mixture with wire whisk until smooth. Chill mixture until partially set.

Fold strawberries and almonds into gelatin. Pour mixture into mold and chill until firm. Unmold onto lettuce-lined serving plate. Arrange whole strawberries around mold. Serve with a sauce dish of strawberry yogurt, if desired.

Makes six-to-eight servings.

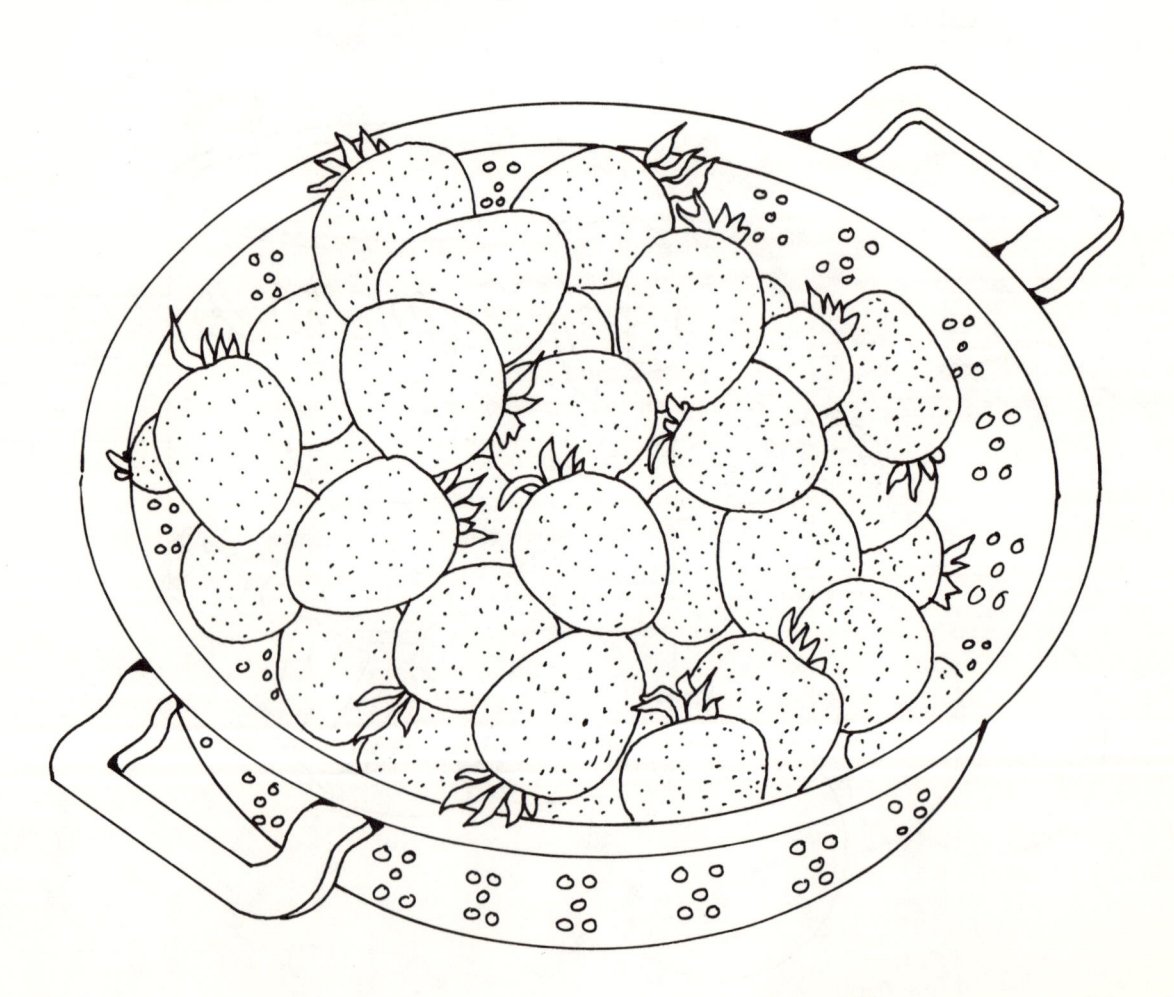

Tomato Ring

2 envelopes unflavored gelatin
1/2 cup hot chicken broth
1 small onion, grated
2 drops Tabasco® sauce
1 tablespoon Worcestershire
1/2 teaspoon celery salt
2 cups tomato juice
1 1/2 tablespoons lemon juice
1 cup mixed cooked vegetables
lettuce leaves
4-cup ring mold

In a saucepan dissolve gelatin in hot chicken broth. Remove saucepan from heat. Add onion, Tabasco®, Worcestershire, and celery salt to gelatin. Stir mixture until well blended. Add tomato juice, lemon juice, and 1 cup cold water to gelatin mixture.

Pour into mold. Chill until firm, about 4 hours. Unmold onto lettuce-lined salad plate. Fill center of mold with mixed vegetables.

Makes six servings.

Annie's Tips

To unmold, run knife carefully around edge of mold. Place serving plate upside-down on top of mold. Invert mold and plate together. A sharp tap on the top of mold is sometimes necessary after this procedure. If the mold sticks, rub it gently with a hot, damp towel, or turn the mold and plate over and repeat the entire process.

INDEX

Apple Raisin Potato Salad, 88
Apple-Raisin Slaw, 72
Asparagus and Mushroom Salad, 46
Avocado Dressing, 16
   peppered, 33
Avocado Gazpacho Salad, 46
avocado-mushroom salad, marinated, 58
Avocado Spinach Salad, 47
Avocado-Tuna Salad Ring, 104
bacon dressing, creamy, 21
bacon salad, mushroom and, 60
Bananas and Pears with Port, 72
Banana Split Salad, 73
Bean Sprout and Cucumber Salad, 47
Bean Sprout and Mushroom Salad, 48
Beet Cucumber Salad Ring, 105
Beet Dressing, 17
Beet Fruit Salad, 74
Beet Salad, 49
beets, tomatoes stuffed with, 65
blue cheese dressing, French-style, 24
blue cheese dressing, zesty, 43
Bologna Salad, 88
Broccoli-Tomato Salad, 50
brown rice toss, chicken and, 89
Buz's Mixed Seafood Salad, 51
Caper Dressing, 18
Cauliflower Salad, 51
Celery Slaw, 52
Cheese and Fruit Salad, 74
Cheese and Lemon Dressing, 19
cheese dressing, two-, 40
Cheese Spinach Salad, 53
Chicken and Brown Rice Toss, 89
Chicken and Ham Salad, 53
Chicken-Potato Salad, 90
Cider Salad Mold, 106

Citrus Dressing, 19
Citrus Salad, 75
   molasses, 81
Cool Cucumber Dressing, 20
Cottage Cheese Peach Salad, 106
crab, pineapple salad with, 81
Crab Salad, 54
Cran-Apple Turkey Salad Mold, 108
Cream Cheese Dressing, 20
Cream Cheese Fruit Salad, 75
Creamy Bacon Dressing, 21
Creamy Salad Dressing, 22
Cucumber and Grape Salad, 109
Cucumber and Shrimp Salad, 55
cucumber dressing, cool, 20
   lemon, 29
Cucumber-Radish Salad, 55
cucumber salad, and bean sprout, 47
Dill Sour Cream Dressing, 22
dip, vegetable salad plate with, 67
dressings, 15-43
   preparation of, 17
   storage of, 34, 37
egg salad, red top, 117
Fines Herbes Vinaigrette, 23
French dressing, honey, 28
French Fry Potato Salad, 92
French Mustard Dressing, 24
French-Style Bean and Potato Salad, 92
French-Style Blue Cheese Dressing, 24
Fresh Fruit Dressing, 26
Frozen Fruitcake Salad, 110
fruit salads, 71-85
Fruit Salad Platter, 76
Fruit Salad with Shrimp, 77

Fruit Squares, *110*
garbanzo bean toss,
   turkey and, *101*
Garden Macaroni Salad, *93*
Gazpacho Salad, *57*
   avocado, *46*
Ginger Cheese Dressing, *26*
Ginger Dressing, *27*
Ginger Summer Salad, *78*
Grapefruit Ring, *112*
Green Salad with Hard-Boiled
   Egg, *57*
ham salad, chicken and, *53*
hard-boiled egg, green
   salad with, *57*
Herbed Sour Cream
   Dressing, *27*
Holiday Fruit Salad, *79*
honey dressing, tomato, *40*
Honey French Dressing, *28*
honey fruit dressing, orange-, *32*
Horseradish Dressing, *29*
Hot Potato Salad, *94*
Japanese Salad, *58*
Lemon-Cucumber Dressing, *29*
Lemon Dressing, *30*
lettuce salad, sesame, *61*
Lime-Walnut Salad, *113*
Macaroni and Cheese Salad, *94*
Macaroni and Cheese Salad
   Ring, *96*
macaroni salad, garden, *93*
Macaroni Slaw, *96*
Marinated Avocado-
   Mushroom Salad, *58*
Marinated Zucchini with
   Tomato Salad, *59*
Mixed Salad, *60*
mixed seafood Salad, Buz's, *51*
Mocha Dressing, *30*
Molasses-Citrus Salad, *81*
Molasses Dressing, *30*

molded salads, *103-121*
Molded Vegetable Salad, *114*
Molded Waldorf Salad, *114*
Mushroom and Bacon Salad, *60*
mushroom salad, and
      asparagus, *46*
   and bean sprout, *48*
naval orange salad, poached, *82*
Orange-Honey Fruit
   Dressing, *32*
Orange salad, naval,
   poached, *82*
Oriental Dressing, *32*
Parmesan Dressing Rosé, *33*
pasta salads, *87-101*
peach salad, cottage
      cheese, *106*
   spiced, *119*
   stuffed, *83*
Pear and Lime Salad
   Mold, *117*
Pear Cucumber Mold, *116*
pear salad, stuffed, *83*
pepper cups, tuna salad in, *66*
Peppered Avocado
   Dressing, *33*
pepper salad, sweet, *64*
Pepper Steak Salad, *97*
Pickled Beet Sour Cream
   Dressing, *34*
Pineapple Salad Dressing, *35*
Pineapple Salad with Crab, *81*
Poached Naval Orange
   Salad, *82*
port, bananas and pears
   with, *72*
potato salad, apple raisin, *88*
   chicken, *90*
   dressing, quick, *36*
   French fry, *92*
   French-style bean and, *92*
   hot, *94*

potatoes, rice, and pasta salads, *87-101*
Quick Potato Salad Dressing, *36*
radish salad, cucumber, *55*
Red Top Egg Salad, *117*
rice toss, chicken and, *89*
rice salad, vegetable, *101*
romaine, special tossed, *62*
rosé dressing, Parmesan, *33*
Sangria Salad, *118*
Seafood Salad, *118*
seafood salad, Buz's mixed, *51*
sea shell salad, tuna-fruit, *99*
Sesame Lettuce Salad, *61*
shrimp salad, and cucumber, *55*
    fruit salad with, *77*
    tomatoes stuffed with, *66*
    vegetable, *68*
slaw, apple-raisin, *72*
    celery, *52*
    dressing, sour cream, *36*
        yogurt, *42*
    macaroni, *96*
sour cream dressing, dill, *22*
    herbed, *27*
    pickled beet, *34*
    slaw, *36*
    tarragon, *39*
Special Green Salad, *62*
Special Tossed Romaine, *62*
Special Yogurt Dressing, *36*
Spiced Peach Salad, *119*
spinach salad, avocado, *47*
    cheese, *53*
Strawberry Delight, *82*
Strawberry Dressing, *37*
Strawberry Yogurt Mold, *120*
Stuffed Peach Salad, *83*
Stuffed Pear Salad, *83*
summer salad, ginger, *78*
Sweetcorn Salad, *98*

Sweet Pepper Salad, *64*
Sweet Yogurt Dressing, *37*
Tangy Tomato Dressing, *37*
Tarragon Sour Cream Dressing, *39*
Tomato-Beef Salad, *64*
tomato dressing, tangy, *37*
Tomatoes Stuffed with Beets, *65*
Tomatoes Stuffed with Shrimp Salad, *66*
Tomato Honey Dressing, *40*
Tomato Ring, *121*
tomato salad, broccoli, *50*
    zucchini with, marinated, *59*
Tomato Salad Rosé, *65*
Tossed Fruit Salad, *84*
Tuna-Fruit Sea Shell Salad, *99*
Tuna Salad in Pepper Cups, *66*
Turkey and Garbanzo Bean Toss, *101*
Two-Cheese Dressing, *40*
Vegetable Rice Salad, *101*
vegetable salad, molded, *114*
Vegetable Salad Plate with Dip, *67*
Vegetable-Shrimp Salad, *68*
vegetables, storage of, *53*
vinaigrette, fines herbes, *23*
Waldorf salad, molded, *114*
White Wine Dressing, *41*
Yam-Fruit Salad, *85*
yogurt dressing, special, *36*
Yogurt Dressing Supreme, *42*
yogurt dressing, sweet, *37*
Yogurt Slaw Dressing, *42*
Zesty Blue Cheese Dressing, *43*
zucchini with tomato salad, marinated, *59*

My Recipes

My Recipes